Advanced Introduction to Behavioral Economics

Elgar Advanced Introductions are stimulating and thoughtful introductions to major fields in the social sciences and law, expertly written by the world's leading scholars. Designed to be accessible yet rigorous, they offer concise and lucid surveys of the substantive and policy issues associated with discrete subject areas.

The aims of the series are two-fold: to pinpoint essential principles of a particular field, and to offer insights that stimulate critical thinking. By distilling the vast and often technical corpus of information on the subject into a concise and meaningful form, the books serve as accessible introductions for undergraduate and graduate students coming to the subject for the first time. Importantly, they also develop well-informed, nuanced critiques of the field that will challenge and extend the understanding of advanced students, scholars and policy-makers.

For a full list of titles in the series please see the back of the book. Recent titles in the series include:

Advanced Introduction to

Behavioral Economics

JOHN F. TOMER

Emeritus Professor of Economics, Manhattan College, USA

Elgar Advanced Introductions

Edward Elgar
PUBLISHING

Cheltenham, UK • Northampton, MA, USA

Published by
Edward Elgar Publishing Limited
The Lypiatts
15 Lansdown Road
Cheltenham
Glos GL50 2JA
UK

Edward Elgar Publishing, Inc.
William Pratt House
9 Dewey Court
Northampton
Massachusetts 01060
USA

A catalogue record for this book
is available from the British Library

Library of Congress Control Number: 2017936573

ISBN 978 1 78471 991 3 (cased)
ISBN 978 1 78471 993 7 (paperback)
ISBN 978 1 78471 992 0 (eBook)

Typeset by Servis Filmsetting Ltd, Stockport, Cheshire
Printed and bound in Great Britain by TJ International Ltd, Padstow

To Hudson, Emma, Milo and Ella

To Hudson, Emma, Lillie and Ella

Contents

Abbreviations

AGM	Arechar, Gachter, and Molleman
BDM	behavioral decision making
BDR	behavioral decision research
BE	behavioral economics
BEs	behavioral economists
BF	behavioral finance
BIT	Behavioural Insights Team
BR	bounded rationality
DF	discount factors
DMT	dual motive theory
DU	discounted utility
EE	experimental economics
EEG	electro-encephalogram
EMH	efficient market hypothesis
ENE	early neoclassical economics
ET	evolutionary theory
fMRI	functional magnetic resonance imaging
H&B	heuristics and biases
MTurk	Amazon Mechanical Turk
NC	new classical economics
NE	neoclassical economics
NEs	neoclassical economists
P/E	price to earnings
PE	psychological economics
PET	positron emission tomography
PT	prospect theory
SEU	subjective expected utility
SMT	Save More Tomorrow
TMS	transcranial magnetic stimulation
UG	ultimatum game
XE	X-efficiency

1   Introduction

Economics is a science, a social science. It is a science whose practices have for a number of decades been contested. The dominant paradigm in economics has for more than sixty years been neoclassical economics (NE). At the heart of NE are 1) the assumption that humans are rational, maximizers of their individual well-being and 2) the proposition that economic behavior can be described very well using mathematical models without the use of psychology or other social sciences. In opposition to the main tenets of NE, behavioral economics (BE) began to emerge in the 1950s. Behavioral economists have sought to create an economic science that has a more realistic conception of human behavior. Moreover, many behavioral economists have worked to create an economics whose methods are less narrow, rigid, and mechanical than those of NE. In the 1950s through to the 1970s, BE had relatively few adherents, but over the years as BE theory and methods advanced, the ranks of behavioral economists have grown greatly. This growth occurred as more and more economists came to recognize that the scientific methods of BE depart substantially from those of NE, and that BE explanations of economic behavior are more realistic owing to the fact that BE combines important insights from psychology and other social sciences with sound economic principles. In recent years, BE has become very prominent and respected and has gained many adherents. It is noteworthy that BE has gained considerable favorable attention as a consequence of the number of behavioral economists who have won the Nobel Prize in Economics for their research. At the same time, more and more economists were coming to recognize that NE models fail to explain important aspects of how humans behave. Another part of the story is that a great many leading young economic researchers now recognize the value of combining a variety of behavioral insights, not just those from psychology, in their theoretical models. And increasingly, empirical research in economics utilizes methods pioneered by behavioral and experimental economists.

Today, if you are an economic researcher, teacher, or student, or are a user of economic research, you need to know about BE. This is very much true even if you are not a specialist in BE. Without sufficient BE knowledge, you will be at a disadvantage unless you are able to understand the most important BE theories and perspectives. In other words, today you need to acquire BE literacy. If becoming literate in BE is your goal, I believe this book is what you need. This book is designed to explain carefully and simply the most important BE theories and perspectives. It is also designed to explain important BE trends and recent developments. If after reading this book you gain a reasonable understanding of BE, it will be much easier for you to go on to acquire greater BE knowledge from texts, references, research articles and books, and intelligent discussions of BE phenomena. Accordingly, this book should be particularly useful for advanced undergraduate students, graduate students, government policymakers, and other professionals who participate in discussions about economics-related matters.

This is to acknowledge two people who were helpful to me in the writing of this book. Len Marowitz grew up in Highland Park, New Jersey, a short distance from my home in the 1950s and 1960s. He now lives in Sacramento, CA. Len is not an economist, but he read every chapter of this book and provided knowledgeable comments on each. I always looked forward to sending my chapters to him and getting his response before digging into the next chapter. Alan Sturmer, Executive Editor at Edward Elgar Publishing Company, invited me to write this book. I appreciated very much his comments on a number of my chapters, his general encouragement, and the opportunities I had to talk with him about Edward Elgar's Advanced Introduction book series and other publishing matters.

2 The scientific practices of economics and the emergence of behavioral economics

Economics as a science

To fully understand behavioral economics (BE), it is necessary to put BE in context and start from the basics. Economics is, of course, a science, a social science. According to John Stuart Mill ((1874) [1968], pp. 120–121), a science is a body of knowledge created by those who are seeking truths about some general area. Scientists in that area investigate pertinent phenomena to discover its laws. The discovered truths often result from careful observation and analysis and involve considerable abstraction. Economic research, as is well known, seeks general truths about production, distribution, consumption, wealth accumulation, and related tasks. Economics is especially concerned with how well or poorly economic systems function in carrying out these tasks. Economics may also concern how to fix economic systems when they are not functioning well.

Scientific practices and what is considered good scientific practice change over time, and this has certainly occurred in economics. It is interesting to note that major changes in economics' scientific practices have been relatively infrequent. According to Michael Mandler (1999, p. 3 as cited in Angner and Loewenstein 2007, p. 4), it is useful to divide the history of modern economics into three main periods: classical, early neoclassical, and postwar neoclassical (or simply neoclassical). Historians date the classical economic period from 1776 to roughly 1890, the early neoclassical period from 1890 to the 1930s, and the neoclassical economics (NE) period from the 1940s to the present. Major changes in the scientific practices of economists occurred in the transitions from one period to the next. Later sections provide important information concerning how the scientific practices of these different periods changed.

Paradigms and scientific revolutions

Thomas Kuhn's *The Structure of Scientific Revolutions* (1970) provides very important perspective and interpretation concerning these fundamental changes over time in scientific practices. One view has been that scientific changes involve a long-term process in which scientific knowledge gradually gets closer and closer to the essential truths. In contrast to this, Kuhn views science as a dynamic and creative process (Preston 2008, p. 5). Accordingly, at certain times in history, fundamental changes occur, changes that are not simply the addition of some new knowledge or information that fits into the framework of what was already known or the correction of mistakes. Such large conceptual changes lead scientists to think very differently about their scientific practice. These large changes are what Kuhn calls scientific revolutions (pp. 2–3).

The concept of paradigm is a key to Kuhn's analysis of scientific change. The paradigm concept is complex because it has a number of related meanings. On the one hand, a paradigm refers to how scientists typically go about their scientific work in a given time period. It is also the scientific model from which initiates are taught; it is an exemplar of scientific practice (Preston 2008, p. 23). Further, a paradigm connotes the scientific approach (a disciplinary matrix) that is consistent with the accepted scientific thought of the time and to which scientists during the period generally conform. A paradigm is also "the entire constellation of beliefs, values, techniques, and so on shared by the members of a given scientific community" (p. 23). Paradigms share symbolic generalizations, models and analogies, virtues and values, and metaphysical principles (p. 39). Although a paradigm can to an extent be considered a conceptual model, it is largely inarticulable; scientists learn the paradigm by example rather than by explicit instruction (pp. 35–36). Paradigms have much to do with the tacit or subliminal aspects of science.

According to Kuhn, in early scientific work, there is a pre-paradigm period in which there is no agreed way of undertaking research. Then at some point when, for example, a researcher makes an important breakthrough that explains the behavior of previously puzzling phenomena, a paradigm may be invented (Preston 2008, p. 11). At this point, other researchers are likely to conduct their scientific activities in conformity to those practices that led to the initial success. Activities undertaken in line with the new paradigm are called normal science. Ideally, the new paradigm is important enough "to attract an enduring group of followers, but at the same time open-ended enough" to motivate further important research (p. 21). The paradigm governing normal scientific practice typically reflects a "kind of consensus characteristic of mature scientific disciplines" (p. 7).

At a later date, problems may occur if researchers' findings include significant results that do not fit with the theories and practices of the existing paradigm. Such findings are called anomalies. The persistence of anomalies "can turn into 'crises,' episodes in which the reigning paradigm begins to lose both its focus and grip" (Preston 2008, p. 11). Ultimately, such crises may substantially undermine the existing paradigm. According to Kuhn, however, scientists do not necessarily abandon the existing paradigm as a result of these problems (p. 48). Scientists "only switch allegiance when there's some more attractive paradigm to switch allegiance to" (p. 48). In other words, scientific revolution only occurs as many scientists adopt the rival, presumably superior, paradigm. During a period of paradigm change, it is likely that relations between those who have adopted the new paradigm and those who are still dedicated to the old paradigm will be acrimonious.

As this book will explain, the scientific practices of BE are sharply different from those of NE. And the BE research that has emerged in the last several decades has become very important. In light of Kuhn's conception of scientific change, it is natural to ask whether BE qualifies as a paradigm, possibly the superior paradigm, that has the potential to succeed the NE paradigm and become the new accepted paradigm that guides a new normal science. At this time, there is no agreement about this. Amitai Etzioni (2011) has cautiously stated his belief that BE has the potential to replace NE and become the new economic paradigm for microeconomics at least. The possibility that BE might become the new paradigm is discussed in Brzezicka and Wisniewski (2014, pp. 360–361). According to Sontheimer (2006, p. 237), "behavioral microeconomics does not constitute a paradigm shift, at least not yet." Angner and Loewenstein's (2007, p. 1) view is that "in recent years, BE has emerged as a *bona fide* subdiscipline of economics [and that it] . . . represents a sharp departure from . . . NE." An important purpose of this book is to carefully examine BE in light of the very long-term changes in the scientific practices of economists, starting with Adam Smith. This book examines both the strengths and weaknesses of BE. On the basis of these, the reader can develop an informed opinion about whether BE is, is becoming, or is likely to become a full-fledged paradigm that will succeed the current paradigm.

Economics and psychology over the years

To appreciate BE and whether BE might be the next economic paradigm, it is necessary to briefly consider some of the main elements of economics' scientific practices and how those have changed from the classical period to the neoclassical period. Because an important aspect of BE involves integrating psychological insights with economic theory, it is particularly important to consider how economics' relationship to psychology has changed over the years.

First, let's consider the psychological insights and perspectives of two important economic thinkers of the classical period, Adam Smith and Jeremy Bentham. Adam Smith is generally understood to be the world's first full-fledged economist. He was also the leading economic thinker and writer of the classical period. So it is important to consider his views on human nature. From his two books, *The Wealth of Nations* [1776] (1976) and *The Theory of Moral Sentiments* [1759] (2002), it is clear that Smith had a broad, multi-faceted, and relatively sophisticated view of human nature (Gilad and Kaish 1986, p. xvii; Angner and Loewenstein 2007, pp. 4–6). Although Smith (1976) is well known for writing about the role that self-interest plays in guiding businesses' behavior, Smith also wrote about how humans are interested in the well-being of others and how people consider others' happiness to be necessary to them (Smith 2002, p. 11). Further:

> Smith's *homo economicus* . . . was a man with a temporal sense, a man with loyalties, a man who clearly understood that he was part of a larger social collective. What Smith's man wanted and needed was the responsibility for making his own decisions and accepting the consequences of those decisions. This responsibility had to be understood as existing in concert with the twin principles of self-love and sympathy, for all were combined in the Smithian calculus. In brief, in modern parlance what was to be maximized by Smith's man was the right of self-determination, while still allowing a place for both moral and social sensibilities and even expressions of altruism. (Perlman and McCann 1998, p. 239)

Thus, a careful reading of Smith's books indicates that he "was deeply interested in the psychological underpinnings of human behavior" (Angner and Loewenstein 2007, p. 6). Furthermore, Ashraf, Camerer, and Loewenstein (2005, p. 140) argue that Smith's work is loaded with insights that anticipate recent developments in BE and, quite possibly, future BE developments.

Another classical economic thinker, Jeremy Bentham, is important with respect to psychology. He developed the doctrine of hedonism and the utilitarian philosophy. According to hedonism, people are motivated to achieve pleasure and avoid pain (Landreth and Colander 2002, pp. 169–70; Canterbery 2001, pp. 69–70). Pleasure is associated with happiness and what is good for the individual and for society. Pain is obviously an undesirable, unhappy outcome. According to Bentham's utilitarian philosophy, individuals should self-interestedly seek to attain the greatest possible pleasure (and happiness) and governments' policies should be aimed at attaining the greatest happiness for the greatest number. A number of other classical thinkers such as John Stuart Mill accepted some aspects of utilitarianism but believed that this philosophy was too dogmatic and narrow and did not reflect the higher aspects of human behavior (Landreth and Colander 2002, p. 169). It should also be noted that classical economists, unlike neoclassical economists, were relatively comfortable writing about mental states and other unobservables; they made frequent reference to cognitive and affective states (Angner and Loewenstein 2007, p. 4).

The economists of the early neoclassical economics (ENE) period undertook careful microeconomic analyses that were very different from the studies of classical economists. Nevertheless, they were unabashedly utilitarians (Angner and Loewenstein 2007, p. 7). One such early neoclassical economist was William Stanley Jevons who "explicitly built his economics on the foundations of hedonic psychology" (p. 6). According to Jevons, "pleasure and pain are undoubtedly the ultimate objects of the Calculus of Economics. To satisfy our wants to the utmost with the least effort . . . in other words, to maximize pleasure, is the problem of economics" (Jevons (1871) [1965], p. 37). ENE economists focused their analyses on utility which is "identical with the addition made to a person's happiness" (p. 45). In their analyses, they heavily relied on introspection to know how much utility was associated with different conscious experiences (Angner and Loewenstein 2007, p. 8). In their view, people behaved rationally in that they weighed the pleasure and pain resulting from different actions and chose the good perceived to give the greatest balance of pleasure over pain (p. 7). But, in the view of ENE economists, people might act irrationally if they did not correctly anticipate the current or future utility resulting from their choices (p. 8).

Postwar neoclassical economics or simply neoclassical economics (NE) emerged in the 1930s and became ascendant by the 1950s. NE economists were strongly motivated by the desire to make economics a fully modern science, one akin to a natural science like physics (Camerer and Loewenstein 2004, p. 5). Accordingly, NE economists wanted to improve economics' scientific practices. In particular, they believed that economics "should focus on behavior only (thereby avoiding references to unobservables such as beliefs, desires, plans, and intentions)" (Angner and Loewenstein 2007, p. 9). They wanted to improve economics' predictive power, and, accordingly, they rejected the use of introspection and referring to conscious states. They were not satisfied with economics' link to psychology, particularly with early neoclassical economics' link to the hedonistic psychology associated with Bentham. Ultimately, NE economists were able to rid economics of practically all its explicit ties to psychology (p. 10). As a result, NE essentially became unidisciplinary, moving toward a theory of greater generality (pp. 11–13). Absent the influence of psychology and other social science disciplines, NE economists describe people's economic behavior as rational, optimizing, and maximizing. "NE economists . . . insist that [people's] deviations from perfect rationality are so small or so unsystematic as to be negligible" (Angner 2012, p. 4). In this NE view, people not only desire to be rational but they also always behave rationally.

Psychology and the emergence of behavioral economics

According to Angner and Loewenstein (2007, p. 3), "behavioral economics emerged in opposition to neoclassical economics" in the postwar years. Why? A very important reason was NE's lack of connection to psychology and other social sciences. Because of this lack of disciplinary connection and because of NE's behavioral assumption of perfect decision making rationality, heterodox economists (including behavioral economists (BEs)) became very critical of NE's lack of behavioral realism. NE's lack of connection to other social sciences is particularly regrettable for those who place a high value on a unified social science or at least on having many viable linkages among the different social sciences. Further, in light of NE's assumption of perfect rationality, economist critics of NE began to recognize an increasing number of anomalous situations in which human behavior was clearly not rational (see, for example, Thaler 1992). Herbert Simon is notable for bringing early attention to the unrealism of the rationality assumption. In Simon's view (1987, p. 221), NE's assumptions about human behavior lack empirical validity. He believed it was the job of behavioral economists to "discover the empirical laws that describe behavior correctly and as accurately as possible" and, based on empirical testing, to modify economic theory. Typically, BEs have drawn on psychological and sociological knowledge to develop theories that are much more realistic than NE theory. The specific ways that BEs have integrated psychology with economics and the types of psychology involved will be explained later.

Scientific methods and the emergence of behavioral economics

The scientific methods of neoclassical economics

Another very important reason for the emergence of BE relates to the scientific methods used by NE economists. The scientific methods of NE are based to a large degree on the precepts of modernistic philosophy of science, notably the idea that science involves a search for absolute universal truths using methods patterned on those of physics. Further, NE fully embraces the positivistic philosophy that "rejects the validity of metaphysical and unprovable statements as scientific knowledge ... [and] regards the human sense experience as the source of scientific knowledge" (Arzlan 2003, p. 6). "Positivistic science emphasizes hypothesis testing and experiments as well as the observable, numerical, non-tacit aspects of the world. Moreover, it involves rigorous, hardnosed rejection of 1) qualitative and intangible aspects, 2) insights deriving from introspection, and 3) historical and cultural aspects" (Tomer 2007, p. 464). Positivistic science like NE has emphasized the use of deductive reasoning, static equilibrium processes, highly mathematical analyses, formal mathematical models, use of advanced statistical decision theory, and models that are sophisticated and elegant (Simon 1992, p. 358). It should also be noted that NE continues to change. According to Landreth and Colander (2002, pp. 382–383), what distinguishes NE in recent years "is its rigid and almost exclusive focus on approaching problems through formal mathematical models .... Modern [NE] economics often seems to take the position that we must discard the idea if it can't be translated into a mathematical model."

Behavioral economists' criticisms of neoclassical economics

BEs (and many other heterodox economists) are critical of the scientific methods of NE. Some BEs reject a large proportion of the methods of NE, while others are only critical of a few of the positivist elements. No doubt, many BEs would agree with Deirdre McCloskey (1994, p. 61) that economics needs methods consistent with a broader, better definition of science. The problem with NE is its very strong commitment to a particular form of positivism. This is reflected in Caldwell's view (1982, pp. 89–92) that positivists are simply too dogmatic about their "refusal to allow subjective, qualitative elements . . . a refusal that [has] artificially limited their analyses and created gaps in their description of science." In Caldwell's view, "the positivist fixation on the objective side of science misses half of a beautiful and complex tale." In essence, the problem with the scientific methods of NE is that "neoclassical economists (NEs) value objective, dispassionate analyses with an almost irrational passion" (p. 89). As McCloskey (1994, p. 5) points out, NE's positivism became "an oppressive rather than a liberating force." Many BEs would presumably agree with McCloskey (1994, pp. 192–193) that knowledge is a complex matter and that there is no simple scientific way to determine what is and is not knowledge. McCloskey emphasizes that good science has the nature of a good conversation in which scientists attempt to persuade their fellow scientists of the relative truth of their propositions. Accordingly, it makes sense that all scientists, including economists, in their attempts to persuade, should use not only facts and logic but stories and metaphors for completed human reasoning (pp. 61–62). "In other words, there is no short, strict list of methods for doing good science" (Tomer 2007, p. 464).

Let's consider the particular criticisms that BEs typically make with respect to NEs' research methods, NEs' sense of scientific discipline, and NEs' behavior toward non-NEs. BEs have criticized NE for its 1) narrowness, 2) rigidity, 3) intolerance, 4) mechanicalness, 5) separateness, and 6) individualism. It is possible to evaluate and rate any scientific discipline on these six dimensions. For example, NE, BE overall, or a particular strand of BE might be rated as high, medium, or low on narrowness. Before going further it is necessary to define these dimensions.

Defining the critical comparison dimensions

Narrowness occurs when an economic discipline restricts its methods and/ or its scope of substantive inquiry. When these restrictions are severe, the economic discipline would be judged to be narrow or high on narrow-ness. Where positivism reigns supreme, the economics is narrow. This is so because, for example, positivism rules out non-quantitative and literary methods to scientific discovery. Where the discipline exclusively uses rigorous testable hypotheses framed in mathematics, positivistic narrowness would be high. Another narrow feature of positivism would be empirical methods that exclude such things as non-quantitative data, author collected data and observations, and surveys . . . [not to mention use of] stories and metaphors. . . . Other significant elements that could make a discipline high on the narrowness dimension . . . include 1) a discipline's unquestioning acceptance of a few core propositions which are excluded from theoretical or empirical examination and . . . 2) a limitation on the kinds of questions that can be investigated. Narrowness may be high when . . . inquiries involving historical and institutional aspects and inquiries involving philosophical or value-laden considerations . . . are excluded. Narrowness would also be high if . . . an economic discipline uses formalistic mathematical-deductivist modeling to the exclusion of other methods.

Rigidity differs from narrowness in that it means not bending or flexible, stiff, hard, and not deviating. If an economic discipline were high in rigidity, this would generally imply a strong attachment (perhaps an irrational attachment) to a particular form of narrowness. Such high rigidity implies that the discipline lacks the ability to be pragmatic and flexible with respect to the methods it uses. Conversely, a discipline low in rigidity can easily adjust its methods according to the type of inquiry involved.

(Tomer 2007, p. 465)

Intolerance refers to a dismissive attitude toward scientific work not conforming to the prescriptions of one's own discipline. Disciplines high on the intolerance dimension are ones whose practitioners are not open-minded, and thus, are relatively hostile and arrogant towards other approaches to economic science. Disciplines low on intolerance have practitioners who are relatively accepting of the methods of other disciplines.

Mechanicalness refers to the degree to which the economy and its actors are viewed by the discipline as behaving in machine-like ways. Disciplines high on mechanicalness are ones whose practitioners tend to conceive of the economy as a complex machine and tend to use machine-like metaphors and concepts such as equilibrium. The practitioners of disciplines low on mechanicalness tend to view the economy as an organic, holistic, evolving, human entity.

Separateness refers to the degree to which an economic discipline is not closely linked or integrated with non-economic disciplines, especially social science disciplines. A discipline high on separateness is one that is relatively self-contained, and thus, separate from other disciplines. A discipline that emphasizes interdisciplinary activity would be judged low on separateness. Individualism implies that the ultimate constituents of the social world are individuals. The individualism of a discipline refers to the degree to which all behavior and events can ultimately be understood as deriving from the characteristics and behavior of individuals. A discipline high on individualism is one where explanations invariably focus on individual decision making behavior. A discipline low on individualism gives much more consideration to individuals as part of collectivities as well as to social and group motivations and behavior. (Tomer, 2007, p. 466)

Conclusions from comparisons

To utilize the six dimensions for comparing NE with BE and its strands, it is necessary to obtain the best possible judgments about these disciplines from knowledgeable scholars. In Tomer (2007, pp. 467–476), I report on the findings of such a comparison. The results for NE (also referred to as mainstream economics) are quite clear. NE is rated high on all six dimensions (narrowness, rigidity, intolerance, mechanical-ness, separateness, and individualism) (p. 476). In contrast, the eight strands of BE (more on these in later sections) are in general far less narrow, rigid, intolerant, mechanical, separate, and individualistic than NE. Some of the BE strands are low on all six dimensions, while a few others have intermediate values on some dimensions, i.e., ratings substantially closer to those of NE than the other BE strands (p. 476). Overall, there is clear evidence that BE is 1) less positivistic than NE (post-positivistic according to Gilad and Kaish (1986, pp. 3, 13)), 2) distinctly different from NE, and 3) much more integrated with other social science disciplines than NE. In other words, BE is arguably better than NE in the way it conducts its scientific practices.

Based on the above, it is not difficult to understand what motivated BE's emergence and why BEs have been very critical of NE. BEs have had very good reasons to be critical of the many objectionable elements of NE. Although, as indicated below, there came to be as many as eight strands of BE, all the strands have to a large extent made similar kinds of criticisms of NE. It is important to note that BE is not a field of economics, a specific economic theory, a theoretical framework, or idea (Gilad and Kaish 1986, pp. xviii–xix; Angner and Loewenstein 2007,

p. 22). BE involves an approach to doing economics, an alternative way to practice economic science. It does not involve an ideology. Ideally, BE involves a commitment to doing good scientific work in economics in a way that is dramatically different from the practices of NE but has links to earlier traditions in economic science.

The strands of behavioral economics

The word, strand, is the right one for thinking about the different traditions of scholarship within BE. A strand is a part that is bound together (as in a rope) to form a whole. BE consists of quite a few strands as well as individual practitioners whose work does not fit neatly into any one of these strands. Because there is enough commonality in these BE strands, they do form a whole. Although eight strands were used in the comparison research cited above, six strands are briefly considered in the following sections. Each of these strands emerged as particular criticisms of NE.

Herbert Simon and bounded rationality

This subsection characterizes the BE of Herbert Simon as well as others following in his footsteps. Simon's main focus was investigating the degree to which decision making is rational and self-interested. Simon was committed "to empirical testing of NE's assumptions on human behavior and to modifying economic theory on the basis of what is found in the testing process" (Simon 1987, p. 221). He sought to replace the motivational assumptions of NE with more accurate assumptions. His term, bounded rationality, relates to all humans' knowledge and capability limitations as well as the complexity and uncertainty of typical real-world situations that humans deal with (p. 222). These factors are what prevent real-world economic actors from behaving according to the rational assumptions of NE theory. Because of bounded rationality, humans have to learn how to make decisions in the real world by employing simplifications, finding new data, adjusting aspirations, developing improved decision making processes, resolving uncertainty, and so on. In other words, humans have to find ways to decide and act that are sufficient, not optimal (Simon 1992, p. 368).

Although Simon was not opposed to mathematics, he made little use of it, and he was certainly not wedded to its use in formalistic modeling (Augier 2003, p. 2). According to Simon, "My attitude towards mathematics and rigor is wholly pragmatic: an argument should be as formal and technical as it needs to be in order to achieve clarity in its statement of issues and its arguments – and no more formal than it needs to be" (as quoted in Augier and March 2003, p. 138).

Simon clearly recognized the intolerant attitudes of neoclassical economists as he was a target of their intolerance. According to Simon, "It was during this period that I began to understand the intensity of [neoclassical] economists' reaction to bounded rationality . . . they were not dealing with it on empirical grounds, but simply rejecting it as irrelevant" (as quoted in Augier 2003, p. 11). Although Simon did not appreciate NEs' intolerance, he was remarkably tolerant of not only neoclassical economists', but also of all economists' use of different methods. Unlike NE, Simon did not believe that economics should be separate from other social science disciplines:

> Understanding Simon's scholarship begins with understanding his embrace of a unified and interdisciplinary behavioral science . . . . He was firmly resistant to demands for disciplinary loyalty. He was one of a post-World War II generation of major scholars who did not see themselves as bound to a single, specific discipline but to the pursuit of topics and methods that were interdisciplinary. (Augier and March 2003, p. 136)

With regard to individualism, although Simon focused a lot of his research on individual decision making, his conception of decision making involved a significant role for social influences on the individual in and outside organizations.

George Katona

George Katona (1980), who was a psychologist by training, along with his collaborators at Michigan University developed a behavioral economic approach that emphasized psychology. Katona was largely interested in understanding consumer behavior and the behavior of the macroeconomy (Sent 2004, p. 741). He emphasized low level theory with a great emphasis on empirical observation of behavior; his approach was far from abstract, positivistic NE (Warneryd 1982, pp. 4, 6, 24, 25). Understanding the performance of the macroeconomy required him to obtain a great deal of information on important subjective, intervening variables. Thus, he made much use of surveys, often involving interviews, to learn about attitudes, aspirations, expectations, optimism/pessimism, social learning/cognition, habituation, and stereotypes. Katona's approach is clearly not narrow, individualistic, or mechanical, and it is very much interdisciplinary.

Harvey Leibenstein and X-efficiency theory

Starting with his first path-breaking article on X-efficiency (XE) in 1966, the thrust of Harvey Leibenstein's XE research has been to develop a conceptual framework for understanding why less than optimal internal efficiency (X-inefficiency) is the usual state of affairs in firms (Leibenstein 1976, 1987; Tomer 1989, 1994). Among the scholars who have done research in this tradition are Shlomo Maital, Morris Altman, Roger Frantz and John Tomer. In my judgment, Leibenstein's research is less narrow than NE but not as broad as the work of Herbert Simon. First, a very important element of XE theory involves questioning the rationality assumption, particularly the idea that people maximize. Second, Leibenstein's work has an element of positivism, but it is not the strict positivism of NE. The style and methods of XE theory are similar to those of NE in the sense that the variables in XE theory are generally quantitative ones, and the theory is in principle testable. Leibenstein's own contribution has been purely theoretical but others can and have done relevant empirical investigations. Note that since XE theory focuses on the underlying relationships inside the firm, there are special challenges to carrying out empirical work. Third, the exposition of XE theory has not used mathematical formalism. Leibenstein has generally used graphs to depict the essential theoretical relationships of his models. This has made his work more accessible than that of the neoclassical economists who use formal mathematical proofs.

Because Leibenstein has relied heavily on the use of partial equilibrium analysis, XE theory could be considered relatively high on the mechanicalness dimension were it not for the somewhat interdisciplinary quality of his research. Leibenstein's general approach involves utilizing key insights from non-economic behavioral disciplines but not explicitly drawing on non-economic research. So his method might be called a limited borrowing approach. Use of these behavioral insights makes XE theory broader in its substance than NE. However, as indicated above, the style and methods of XE theory are in some respects not far from that of NE. What Leibenstein appears to have done is to present his novel behavioral ideas in a language familiar to neoclassical economists. Leibenstein's XE theory has an interdisciplinary element but it is certainly not fully integrated with social science disciplines like psychology and sociology.

Leibenstein's analysis focuses very much on the individual, an individual who is self-interested, but generally not fully rational. The "man" in Leibenstein's economics is a social man in the sense of being constrained by commitments, social obligations, conventions, identifications, and attitudes about cooperation. Psychological man is also present, man with achievement need, contaminating emotion, and with motivation/enthusiasm affected by the degree of bureaucracy. Self-actualizing man is, however, not present here.

Psychological economics

Daniel Kahneman is the acknowledged leader of another important strand of behavioral economics that challenges economists' model of rational choice. He, along with his close collaborator and frequent coauthor the late Amos Tversky and many others, does research in the psychological economics tradition. Psychological economics (PE) focuses particularly on the cognitive functioning of the human mind and why people are prone to make predictable errors in their judgments and decision making. Compared to Simon's research, PE tends to focus on smaller decisions and on less complex situations in order to isolate specific types of human cognitive bias. Their empirical research often takes place in laboratory settings that allow controlled experimentation. Leading practitioners of PE include Colin Camerer, Ernst Fehr, David Laibson, George Loewenstein, Matthew Rabin, and Richard Thaler.

PE researchers have found, for example, that humans have a "systematic tendency toward unrealistic optimism about the time it takes to complete projects" (the planning fallacy) (Thaler and Sunstein 2009, p. 7). Humans also typically "have a strong tendency to go along with the status quo or default option" (status quo bias) (pp. 7–8). PE researchers have identified many more systematic departures from the economically rational decision making behavior postulated by NE. These and many other systematic errors or biases identified by PE researchers are a result of how the human mind works ("the design of the machinery of cognition") (Kahneman 2011, pp. 3–8).

PE is less narrow than NE but more narrow than the BE strands identified with Herbert Simon and George Katona. According to Colin Camerer and George Loewenstein (2004, p. 7), PE research tends to follow a standard recipe: 1) identify normative assumptions or models used in NE, 2) identify anomalies, clear violations of the assumptions or models, 3) use the anomalies as inspiration to create alternative theories that generalize existing models, and 4) construct models of economic behavior using the revised assumptions, test them, and derive new implications. As part of this PE process, the core NE assumptions of self-interest, rationality, and self-control are challenged (Rabin 2002, p. 658). Nevertheless, PE's basic methods do not represent a radical departure from NE. PE, in Rabin's view, "continues to employ NE methods construed broadly" (p. 658). The purpose of much PE research is, thus, simply to "modify one or two assumptions in standard theory in the direction of greater psychological realism" (Camerer and Loewenstein 2004, p. 3). It follows that PE shares much of the positivism of NE. Correspondingly, PE research tends to focus on relatively tangible, quantifiable factors and to limit its consideration of intangible, qualitative, holistic aspects. PE is "built on the premise that NE methods are great . . . [and] that most NE assumptions are great" (Rabin 2002, p. 658).[1] PE is in a sense based on NE's concept of rational decision making because it defines decision making error as a departure from standard economic notions of rationality (Angner and Loewenstein 2007, p. 29). Although some PE practitioners utilize mathematical methods extensively to describe behavior or show where NE is in error, PE is generally less mathematical than NE. Rabin (p. 672) finds the mathematical formalism of NE to be a "necessary evil." On the one hand, it is evil because it entails "highly simplified and stylized models of human cognition, preferences, and behavior that, in every instance, omit a tremendous amount of psychological reality." On the other, it is necessary in order "to formulate precise and testable hypotheses."

The empirical studies of PE have been to a large extent oriented to documenting how human behavior typically violates the patterns of behavior predicted by NE's subjective expected utility model (Angner and Loewenstein 2007, p. 35). It should be noted that PE currently embraces a full range of empirical methods including all the empirical methods of NE as well as laboratory and field experimentation, use of field data, computer simulation, surveys, and even brain scans (Camerer and Loewenstein 2004, p. 7). Psychological economists like to think of themselves as "methodological eclectics" (p. 8).

PE is much less mechanical than NE owing to its use of other social science disciplines, especially psychology. PE is low in separateness compared to NE, but it is not nearly as interdisciplinary as Herbert Simon's work. PE's most important link with other disciplines is with behavioral decision research, a subfield of psychology (Angner and Loewenstein 2007, p. 28). One interesting new development is PE's connection with neuroscience to develop neuroeconomics (p. 38). Lastly, PE is much less individualistic than NE, as practitioners of PE recognize that human behavior may not be self-interested or strictly rational, and they recognize important social influences on individual decision making.

George Akerlof and behavioral macroeconomics

George Akerlof's (2002) Nobel prize lecture summarizes key elements of behavioral macroeconomics, especially his own contributions. Akerlof's dream has been to develop behavioral macroeconomics in the original spirit of Keynes' General Theory, a behavioral macroeconomics, however, which is less based on intuition and more explicitly based on sound psychology and sociology. Moreover, in doing this, he has hoped "to strengthen macroeconomic theory by incorporating assumptions honed to the observation of such behaviors" (p. 411).

A strong motive for developing behavioral macroeconomics is that the New Classical (NC) macroeconomics (a branch of NE) which emerged in the late 1960s has failed to satisfactorily explain six important macroeconomic phenomena (Akerlof 2002, pp. 411–412). The six phenomena are: 1) the existence of involuntary unemployment, 2) the obvious impact of monetary policy on output and employment, 3) the failure of deflation to accelerate when unemployment is high, 4) the prevalence of undersaving for retirement, 5) the excessive volatility of stock prices relative to their fundamentals, and 6) the stubborn persistence of a self-destructive underclass (p. 412). For each of these six important phenomena, Akerlof and other behavioral macroeconomists have developed analyses "incorporating realistic assumptions grounded in psychological and sociological observation" (p. 413); these provide very satisfactory explanations of the phenomena and explain why the NC explanations are flawed. For example, behavioral macroeconomic explanations of involuntary unemployment utilize three important considerations: "1) reciprocity (gift exchange from anthropology), 2) fairness (equity theory from psychology), and 3) adherence to group norms (reference group theory in sociology and theory of group formation in psychology)" (p. 415). In contrast to NC economists, behavioral macroeconomists appreciate that price and wage levels are typically inflexible downward. The keys to understanding why this is often the case are important psychological insights that help explain why workers resist nominal wage cuts and why firms use rules-of-thumb in price setting (pp. 417–420).

Akerlof's behavioral macroeconomics is much less narrow than NE. First, unlike in NE, Akerlof's research does not include unquestioning acceptance of core propositions such as maximizing utility and profit. Second, there is considerable openness to research questions and issues which NE has not been open to. Third, Akerlof's research is not characterized by the use of formalistic mathematical modeling.

As the above has indicated, the work of Akerlof and that of other behavioral macroeconomists is very much interdisciplinary, and thus, much less separate than NE. Akerlof has argued that important behaviors studied by psychologists and sociologists such as "reciprocity, fairness, identity, money illusion, loss aversion, herding, and procrastination help explain the significant departures of real-world economies from the competitive, [NE] . . . model" (Akerlof 2002, p. 428). It should be noted that Akerlof's behavioral macroeconomic work has some close connections to the microeconomic work of BEs in the PE strand, especially insofar as it utilizes insights concerning departures from rational economic decision making.

Richard Nelson, Sidney Winter and evolutionary theory

Richard Nelson and Sidney Winter (see, for example, 1982) have pioneered in the use of evolutionary theory to explain the processes of economic progress or development. Their theorizing borrows the evolutionary idea from biology, especially Darwin's notion of natural selection involving differential rates of survival. They focus on firms' regular, predictable behavioral patterns which they call routines (p. 14). Routines are analogous to genes in that the better ones are selected due to the survival and prospering of firms containing these (Nelson and Winter 2002, pp. 25, 30). This evolutionary theory is highly compatible with the hypothesis of an industry life cycle in which the rise and development of a new technology goes hand-in-hand with a dramatic change in the number of firms in the market (p. 35). Many firms enter in the early, uncertain stages, and many later exit as the industry matures. Evolutionary theory has many applications to and implications for understanding technological change processes.

Evolutionary theory (ET) is in my judgment relatively low in narrowness. ET is open to a wider range of research methods than NE, and it is less positivistic. ET does not use formalist mathematical models, and it is relatively open to investigation of its core economic propositions as well as being open to inquiries related to historical and institutional aspects.

ET is in my judgment also low in mechanicalness. First, it makes limited use of mathematics. Second, there is in ET a recognition that while human behavior frequently conforms to regular patterns or routines, humans generally do not behave in a maximizing way. ET is much less individualistic than NE. ET does not depend on individualistic explanations of behavior. ET is very compatible with concepts in the field of organizational behavior. Further, ET is strongly interdisciplinary; its connections with modern organizational theory, business strategy, business history, and cognitive psychology are especially strong.

Other behavioral economic strands

Arguably, besides the six described above, there are a number of other BE strands. A strong case can be made that behavioral finance (BF) is a separate strand of BE. This is because BF has very close connections to BE, especially to psychological economics. And many BF practitioners are also BEs by virtue of their research and their economics PhDs. On the other hand, it can be argued that BF is a topic in finance that deals with the behavior of financial markets. Here BF is not considered a BE strand. However, BF is covered in some detail later in this book because of its strong relationship to BE.

The topic of experimental economics, especially the work of Vernon Smith and his collaborators, is another candidate to be a strand of BE. It is a candidate because laboratory experiments have become widely used in economics, especially by BEs and BF practitioners. However, the essence of experimental economics is an empirical method. It is not for the most part a substantive field of inquiry (Angner and Loewenstein 2007, pp. 38–39). So it is not included here as a BE strand. Nevertheless, experimental economics and its growth are an important part of the story of BE. Therefore, it will be covered in some detail later in this book.

Perhaps, there are other strands of BE that have not been identified here, not to mention individual scholars whose work does not fit neatly into any one of the BE strands identified in this chapter.

Differences within behavioral economics

Sent (2004, pp. 740–750) distinguishes "old behavioral economics" from "new behavioral economics." Briefly, old BE is that of Herbert Simon and bounded rationality, George Katona, Harvey Leibenstein and X-efficiency theory, Richard Nelson and Sidney Winter's evolutionary theory, a group at Oxford University, and a handful of others (pp. 740–742). New BE is mainly psychological economics but it might include the Akerlof strand and the research of a few other prominent BEs. Old BE certainly came into being before new BE, but the distinction between the two relates more to their respective scientific methods, perspectives, and theoretical frameworks than to the dates of publication of old and new BE authors' important research. Sent points out that new BE is situated squarely within the mainstream of economics (p. 749), contributes important psychological realism to economics, and has sharp testable predictions. These and related attributes no doubt account for new BE's success relative to old BE in gaining adherents.

Whereas new BE has considerable ties to the economic mainstream and new BEs have a greater comfort level with mainstream economics, old BEs are more dissatisfied with NE and have a strong desire to develop an alternative to mainstream economics. Further, it is noteworthy that leading new BE researchers have not been particularly tolerant of old BEs and have typically had dismissive attitudes toward economists in the old BE camp. This is true even for someone with a high status in old BE like Herbert Simon. His theories are not respected by many PEs, and his ideas are missing from recent PE writings (Sent 2004, p. 750). At the heart of the matter is new BEs' view that "these economists [old BEs] appear to have had little influence on the direction of economics as a whole" (Angner and Loewenstein 2007, p. 25). (For a complete historical account of new BE's rise to prominence, see Heukelom (2014)). It is also noteworthy that quite a few economists who started their careers in one of the strands of old BE have over the years become more receptive to the theories and perspectives of other strands (including those of new BE). However, the same cannot be said for new BE practitioners; they do not seem to have increased their receptivity to the scientific practices and theories of old BEs. Therefore, the recent situation in BE might be characterized as a moderate, but imperfect, pluralism (Sent 2005, p. 754). Will the dominance of PE within BE continue or even increase? Or will BE as a whole become more pluralistic and integrated? The answers are not clear.

Behavioral economics: the next economic paradigm?

Might BE become the superior paradigm with the potential to replace the NE paradigm? The answer to this question is also not clear. On the one hand, PE is very strong in its use of psychology to improve the realism of economics. But PE is too closely tied to the NE paradigm and its scientific practices to become more than an excellent subdiscipline of NE. On the other hand, many of the scholars whose work is in the strands of old BE, particularly the Herbert Simon strand, appreciate to a much greater extent than PEs the need to change the scientific practices of economics, particularly the positivistic ones. If BE can utilize the best of PE, integrate it with the insights of old BE, and simultaneously become less narrow, rigid, intolerant, mechanistic, individualistic, and separate, BE might then have the potential to be the superior paradigm with the opportunity to replace NE. Whether that potential will be realized or not cannot be determined at this time. Nevertheless, the chapters that follow will explore the many specific important contributions of BE in order to gain insight regarding whether a process leading to paradigm change is occurring now or could occur in the near future.

NOTE
1 Rabin's statement seems to be an exaggeration that I suspect not many BEs (even PEs) would agree with.

References

Akerlof, George. 2002. "Behavioral Macroeconomics and Macroeconomic Behavior," *American Economic Review*, 92(3), June, 411–433.

Angner, Erik. 2012. *A Course in Behavioral Economics*. New York: Palgrave Macmillan.

Angner, Erik and Loewenstein, George. 2012. "Behavioral Economics" (January 14, 2007), in Uskali Maki (ed) *Handbook of the Philosophy of Science: Philosophy of Economics*, Amsterdam: Elsevier, 641–690. Available at SSRN.

Arzlan, D. 2003. "Postmodernism, Keynesian Uncertainty and Rational Expectations: A Methodological Approach," Paper presented at the Eastern Economic Association Conference in New York City on February 22.

Ashraf, Nava, Camerer, Colin F. and Loewenstein, George. 2005. "Adam Smith, Behavioral Economist," *Journal of Economic Perspectives*, 19, 131–145.

Augier, Mie. 2003. "Will the Real Herbert Simon Please Stand Up? (Or, Behavioral Economics: Hopes for the Past; Lessons from the Future," Paper Presented at the Eastern Economic Association Conference in New York City on February 23.

Augier, Mie and March, James G. 2003. "The Economic Psychology of Herbert Simon: Introduction to a Special Issue," *Journal of Economic Psychology*, 24(2), April, 135–141.

Brzezicka, Justyna and Wisniewski, Radoslaw. 2013. "Homo Oeconomicus and Behavioral Economics," *Contemporary Economics*, 8(4), 353–364.

Caldwell, Bruce J. 1982. *Beyond Positivism: Economic Methodology in the Twentieth Century*. London: Allen and Unwin.

Camerer, Colin F. and Loewenstein, George. 2004. "Behavioral Economics: Past, Present, Future," in Camerer, Colin F., Loewenstein, George and Rabin, Matthew (eds) *Advances in Behavioral Economics*. New York: Princeton University Press, 3–51.

Canterbery, E. Ray. 2001. *A Brief History of Economics: Artful Approaches to the Dismal Science*. London: World Scientific.

Etzioni, Amitai. 2011. "Behavioral Economics: Toward a New Paradigm," *American Behavioral Scientist*, 55(8), 1099–1119.

Gilad, Benjamin and Kaish, Stanley. 1986. *Handbook of Behavioral Economics: Behavioral Microeconomics*. London: Jai Press.

Heukelom, Floris. 2014. *Behavioral Economics: A History*. New York: Cambridge University Press.

Jevons, W. Stanley. 1871 [1965]. *The Theory of Political Economy*. 5th Edition. New York: A. M. Kelley.

Kahneman, Daniel. 2011. *Thinking Fast and Slow*. New York: Farrar, Straus, and Giroux.

Katona, George. 1980. *Essays on Behavioral Economics*. Ann Arbor, MI: Institute for Social Research.

Kuhn, Thomas S. 1970. *The Structure of Scientific Revolutions*. Chicago: University of Chicago Press.

Landreth, Harry and Colander, David C. 2002. *History of Economic Thought*. 4th Edition. Boston: Houghton Mifflin.

Leibenstein, Harvey. 1976. *Beyond Economic Man: A New Foundation for Microeconomics*. Cambridge, MA: Harvard University Press.

Leibenstein, Harvey. 1987. *Inside the Firm: The Inefficiencies of Hierarchy*. Cambridge, MA: Harvard University Press.

Mandler, Michael. 1999. *Dilemmas in Economic Theory: Persisting Foundational Problems of Microeconomics*. New York: Oxford University Press.

McCloskey, Deirdre N. 1994. *Knowledge and Persuasion in Economics*. Cambridge: Cambridge University Press.

Mill, John Stuart. 1874 [1968]. "On the Definition of Political Economy; and On the Method of Investigation Proper to It," in *Essays on Some Unsettled Questions of Political Economy*. New York: Augustus M. Kelley, 120–164.

Nelson, Richard R. and Winter, Sidney G. 1982. *An Evolutionary Theory of Economic Change*. Cambridge, MA: Harvard University Press.

Nelson, Richard R. and Winter, Sidney G. 2002. "Evolutionary Theorizing in Economics," 16(2), Spring, 23–46.

Perlman, M. and McCann, C.R. 1998. *The Pillars of Economic Understanding, Vol. 1: Ideas and Traditions*. Ann Arbor, MI: University of Michigan Press.

Preston, John. 2008. *Kuhn's The Structure of Scientific Revolutions: A Reader's Guide*. New York: Continuum.

Rabin, Matthew. 2002. "A Perspective on Psychology and Economics," *European Economic Review*, 46, 657–685.

Sent, Esther-Mirjam. 2004. "Behavioral Economics: How Psychology Made Its (Limited) Way Back Into Economics," *History of Political Economy*, 36(4), 735–760.

Simon, Herbert. 1987. "Behavioral Economics," in Eatwell, John, Milgate, Murray and Newman, Peter (eds) *The New Palgrave: A Dictionary of Economics*. New York: Stockton Press, 221–225.

Simon, Herbert. 1992. "Nobel Prize Lecture," in Lindbeck, Assar (ed) *Nobel Lectures, Economic Sciences, 1969–1980*. London: World Scientific, 335–371.

Smith, Adam. [1759] 2002. *The Theory of Moral Sentiments*. K. Haakonssen (ed) Cambridge: University of Cambridge Press.

Smith, Adam. [1776] 1976. *An Inquiry into the Nature and Causes of the Wealth of Nations*. Chicago: University of Chicago Press.

Sontheimer, Kevin. 2006. "Behavioral Versus Neoclassical Economics: Paradigm Shift or Generalization," in Altman, Morris (ed) *Handbook of Contemporary Behavioral Economics: Foundations and Developments*. Armonk, NY: M.E. Sharpe, Chapter 12, pp. 237–257.

Thaler, Richard H. 1992. *The Winner's Curse: Paradoxes and Anomalies of Economic Life*. New York: Free Press.

Thaler, Richard H. and Sunstein, Cass R. 2009. *Nudge: Improving Decisions About Health, Wealth, and Happiness*. Revised. New York, Penguin Books.

Tomer, John F. 1989. "Review of Harvey Leibenstein's *Inside the Firm*," *Journal of Economic Behavior and Organization*, 12(1), August, 153–157.

Tomer, John F. 1994. "Leibenstein, Harvey," in Hodgson, G., Samuels, W. and Tool, M. (eds) *The Elgar Companion to Institutional and Evolutionary Economics*. Volume 2. Aldershot, UK and Brookfield, VT: Edward Elgar Publishing.

Tomer, John F. 2007. "What Is Behavioral Economics?" *Journal of Socio-Economics*, 36, 463–479.

Warneryd, Karl-Erik. 1982. "The Life and Work of George Katona," *Journal of Economic Psychology*, 2, 1–31.

3   The practices and content of the bounded rationality strand

Introduction

In Chapter 2, the key characteristics of six strands of behavioral economics (BE) were briefly considered. To gain a better understanding of BE and its potential as a new economic paradigm, it is necessary to consider more fully the variety of practices and contributions of BE. This chapter focuses on the BE of bounded rationality, the BE associated closely with the work of Herbert Simon. The purpose here is to examine the contributions and practices of this BE strand and contrast them with those of neoclassical economics (NE). Later chapters will focus on other strands and other contributions of BEs. Hopefully, these chapters will provide the reader with enough knowledge and insight to form an educated idea about the relative merits of BE and NE and whether BE has a chance to become the superior paradigm that might one day supplant NE.

Herbert Simon

The scientific practices and orientation of the bounded rationality (BR) strand of BE reflect Herbert Simon's character in many respects. Therefore, it is important to understand the essence of his role with respect to economics. Herbert Simon (1916–2001) was a social scientist whose practices and interests differed sharply from those of most economists. As indicated in Chapter 2, Simon was committed to interdisciplinary social science. This is indicated by the fact that Simon made important contributions to economics, psychology, political science, sociology, administrative theory, public administration, organization theory, computer science, cognitive science, and philosophy (Augier and March 2002, pp. 1–2). He resisted disciplinary loyalty. As he said, "If you see any one of these disciplines dominating you, you join the opposition and you fight it for a while" (p. 2). Nevertheless, the field of economic behavior and organization (along with psychology) was very important to him. And although he failed to achieve the influence on economics that he sought, he did win the Nobel Prize in Economic Science in 1978 (Simon 1992; Augier and March 2002, p. 4). Simon's multidisciplinary interests were all related to one core interest, understanding human decision making (p. 15). "His quest to understand human decision making as it actually occurred led him to contribute" to many fields (p. 3). According to Simon, "'the big problem for me . . . was to reconcile the way that decisions were actually made in organizations with the way that economists pretended that they were made'" (p. 4). His research agenda focused on how humans reason and decide when it is not possible for them to be rational in the manner postulated by NE. His disillusionment with NE led him to challenge the key elements of the NE view of rational decision making (p. 2). With respect to the economics discipline, Simon was in accord with Alfred Marshall who thought of economics as part of the study of man, and thus, as a psychological science (Simon 1992, p. 343). In Simon's view, it was unfortunate that economics, that is, NE, "has focused on just one aspect of Man's character, his reason, and particularly on the application of that reason to problems of allocation in the face of scarcity" (p. 343).

Rational decision making

Like any economist, Herbert Simon appreciated rational decision making. But what neoclassical economists (NEs) define as rational is not the same as the general (and Simon's) definition of rational. According to the dictionary (or general) definition, rationality in decision making signifies "agreeable to reason, not absurd, preposterous, extravagant, foolish"; it is decision making that is "intelligent and sensible." In contrast, NE rationality in decision making means maximizing (or optimizing), that is, unfailingly choosing the absolute best alternative (Simon 1978, p. 2). The NE rational decision maker is assumed to have all the knowledge and computational skill necessary to enable him/her to calculate the utility of alternative choices (Simon 1955, p. 99). NE rationality means that decision makers always choose the alternative providing maximum utility. Although Simon understood that this NE conception was very unrealistic, he had to admit that the "classical theory of omniscient rationality is strikingly simple and beautiful" (Simon 1992, p. 347).

The formal NE theory of decision making when uncertainty is present is called subjective expected utility (SEU) theory. It assumes that the decision maker can assign a number measuring his liking to any possible alternative, that there is a well-defined set of alternatives, and that the decision maker knows the probability of occurrence of each alternative. The latter implies no unanticipated consequences. The theory further assumes that the decision maker is able to choose the alternative that maximizes the expected utility value (Simon 1983, pp. 12–13; Simon 1955, p. 103). The theory is impressive. Unfortunately, as Simon has pointed out, "the SEU theory has never been applied – with or without the largest computers – in the real world (Simon 1983, p. 14). The only exceptions to this are choice situations where the degree of complexity is far below that in real world human choice situations (p. 17; Simon 1955, p. 104). Thus, in Simon's view, "decision makers, no matter how badly they want to do so, simply cannot apply the SEU model" (p. 17). This is especially true because to maximize utility as in the SEU theory, humans would require not only unlimited cognitive capabilities but also unlimited noncognitive capabilities such as emotional and motivational capabilities (Selten 2001, pp. 14–15).

As indicated earlier, Herbert Simon disagreed with the NE concept of rational decision making. For Simon, rationality in decision making meant choosing in a reasoned, purposeful, intentionally rational manner (Augier and March 2002, p. 5). Such decision making is functional in the sense that it contributes to achieving a person or organization's goals. Simon understood that humans' limited cognitive capacities did not allow them to maximize except in extremely simple situations. Nevertheless, in his view, "'reasonable men' reach 'reasonable' conclusions in circumstances where they have no prospect of applying classical models of . . . rationality" (Simon 1978, p. 14). Consistent with the above, Simon distinguished between substantive and procedural rationality. Substantive rationality relates to the degree to which a choice outcome is the best or maximum one given the actor's goals (Simon 1976, pp. 130–131). Procedural rationality relates to the process of reason and deliberation used to find a solution to a problem. "Behavior is procedurally rational when it is the outcome of appropriate deliberation" (p. 131). Decision making is not rational in a procedural sense if the process involves an "impulsive response . . . without an adequate intervention of thought" (p. 131). In Simon's view, the best that humans can do is to achieve a relatively high degree of procedural rationality that produces good enough decisions.

In developing an alternative model of decision making, Simon started with the basics of conventional decision theory. In other words, Simon realized that decision makers confront choice alternatives, payoffs to these choices, possible future states of the world, and information about the probability distributions associated with choice outcomes (Augier and March 2002, p. 7). Simon further realized that decision makers lack the computational power to deal with the decision complexity involved. Therefore, Simon believed that decision makers, of necessity, need to utilize simplified decision procedures. First, they simplify by choosing from a limited set of alternatives, a subset of the universe of alternatives (Simon 1955, p. 102). Second, they use selective heuristics or rules of thumb that enable them to explore promising subsets of alternatives (Simon 1976, p. 136). Third, they generally examine the chosen subset of alternatives sequentially, one alternative at a time (Simon 1955, 110). Fourth, they do what Simon called satisficing. That is, they search until they find a satisfactory solution alternative, one that is "good enough"; they select that one, thus ending the search (Augier and March 2002, p. 7). The goal of the search is not to find the best alternative; it is only to find a good alternative (pp. 7–8). The selected alternative is the first one that meets the decision maker's aspiration level. In Simon's view, a person's aspiration level may change. The general principle is that aspiration levels rise when it is easy to discover satisfactory alternatives, and they fall when it is difficult to discover satisfactory alternatives (Simon 1955, p. 111).

Simon recognized that there is another important element in good decision making. "A great deal of the success of human beings in arriving at correct decisions is due to the fact that they have good intuition or good judgment" (Simon 1983, pp. 23–24). In the popular imagination, some people just have good intuition and judgment and others do not. In Simon's view, it is not that simple. It is certainly true that sometimes people arrive at problem solutions suddenly. They have an "aha" experience. "There is no doubt of the genuineness of the phenomenon. Moreover, the problem solutions people reach when they have these experiences and make an intuitive judgment, frequently are correct" (p. 25). One example is the quick, strong decisions made by chess masters. In Simon's view, these rapid intuitive judgments occur when decision makers have a great amount of experience that enables them to recognize and retrieve from memory all the patterns learned over years of experience (pp. 25–27). In other words, the "'aha' experiences happen only to people who possess the appropriate [experience and] knowledge" (p. 27), people who have prepared minds. In Simon's view, it takes a long time "to prepare a mind for world-class creative performance" in chess and other endeavors (p. 27) or even to achieve

reasonably good intuitive judgment in business and household decision making.

Bounded rationality

Herbert Simon (1987, p. 222) used the term "bounded rationality"
to refer to the "whole range of limitations on human knowledge and
computation that prevent real world actors from behaving like economic man." Besides the satisficing and intuitive decision making
described above, the following behaviors are examples of boundedly
rational decision making. First, one way humans avoid calculation in
decision making is to use conventions (Simon 1987, p. 222). This is
particularly so when social phenomenon are involved. For example,
business decisions on salaries and personal decisions on savings are
often made based on socially accepted conventions rather than some
form of rational calculation. Typically, businesses set their managerial
salary levels in close conformity to what other businesses are doing
and what is considered acceptable to the public. Second, when making
decisions such as buying a car, people generally focus their attention
only on the parts of their life most directly related to their decision,
e.g., vehicular transportation, and they tend to neglect all other aspects
of their life (Simon 1983, pp. 19–20). Third, owing to their cognitive
limitations, humans generally do not develop detailed scenarios of the
future with associated probability distributions (p. 18). A fourth example of bounded rationality is adaptation and learning. This occurs when
people and businesses gradually change their choices based on what
choices have worked more or less well in the past (Simon 1959, p. 271).
Businesses, for example, generally set initial performance targets based
on their aspiration levels and then gradually adjust these targets as they
adapt to experience.

Simon's metaphor of the pair of scissors is arguably the best way to
explain the bounded rationality concept. One blade of the scissors is
the cognitive limitations of humans; the other blade is the structure
of the environment (Gigerenzer and Selten 2001, p. 4). Structure of
the environment refers to the nature of the decision making situation (the people, animals, institutions, etc.). The essence of bounded
rationality is the idea that "minds with limited time, knowledge, and
other resources can nevertheless [be] successful [in decision making]
by exploiting structures in their environments" (p. 4). Thus, if the first
blade of the scissors which is related to mental capacity fits well with

the second which is related to the environment, the scissors work well, and the result is good enough decisions without great cost. In this case, humans with ordinary cognitive abilities using appropriate rules of thumb (heuristics) and decision making procedures (ones well suited to their environments) can realize favorable decision making outcomes.

Gerd Gigerenzer and his research colleagues are strong advocates of the view that humans' use of boundedly rational decision making methods can often be successful even if the decision outcomes are far from optimal. Optimum decision making is, of course, the goal of traditional models of inference whose methods involve integrating all available information, weighting it, and combining it in a computationally expensive way (Gigerenzer and Goldstein 1996, p. 652). Boundedly rational decision making does not attempt to integrate all available information; it is based on limited knowledge, memory search, and intelligent guesses about unknown features of the world (p. 652). Boundedly rational decision methods are ones that a human mind can actually carry out when they have limited time and knowledge. Boundedly rational decision makers often use informed guesses and go beyond the information given. Boundedly rational decision making makes much use of heuristics, the shortcut decision processes that are useful for solving difficult problems (Berg and Gigerenzer 2010, p. 157). "By ignoring information, a heuristic can be more accurate in making predictions in a changing and uncertain world than [an optimizing strategy]" (p. 157). In contrast to decision making methods that attempt to achieve optimal outcomes and are universally applicable, boundedly rational methods use decision processes that are designed to work well only with specific types of decision environments (p. 149). Ecological rationality is the type of rationality that can be realized when the chosen decision processes function well in conjunction with particular classes of environments. Such boundedly rational decision methods are satisficing, simple, intelligent, fast, frugal, and capable of making near optimal inferences to the extent that they take advantage of regularities in the structure of the decision environment (Berg and Gigerenzer 2010, p. 651; Gigerenzer and Selten 2001, p. 7). The results of using boundedly rational decision making methods that use "simple and robust heuristics can match or even outperform a specific optimizing strategy" (p. 4). Also note that besides using information, these decision making methods may also make use of emotions and social influences to obviate the need for information and calculation (p. 9).

Has the theory of bounded rationality been successful? Yes and no. On the one hand, "a significant number of empirical studies have been carried out that show actual decision making to conform reasonably well with the assumptions of bounded rationality but not with the assumptions of perfect rationality" (Simon 1992, p. 357). On the other hand, despite the reasonable prospect that theories of bounded rationality would become a significant part of mainstream economics, that did not happen. "First, there was a vigorous reaction that sought to defend classical theory from behavioralism" on the grounds that the scientific methods of Simon and his BE colleagues were inferior to those of NEs (p. 357). "Second, the rapid spread of mathematical knowledge and competence in the economic profession permitted the classical theory, especially when combined with statistical decision theory and the theory of games, . . . to develop to new heights of sophistication and elegance . . ." (p. 358). As a consequence, these developments "have absorbed . . . [economists'] energies and postponed encounters with the inelegancies of the real world" (p. 358). Thus, in Simon's view, the economics profession was not intellectually prepared during the 1960s, 1970s, and 1980s at least to accept the bounded rationality concept, not to mention many other aspects of BE. Nevertheless, Simon was clear about the importance of bounded rationality:

> We do understand today many of the mechanisms of human rational choice. We do know how the information processing system called Man, faced with complexity beyond his ken, uses his information processing capacities to seek out alternatives, to calculate consequences, to resolve uncertainties, and thereby – sometimes, not always – to find ways of action that are sufficient unto the day. (Simon 1992 p. 368)

Conclusion

Herbert Simon was clearly a great scholar, economist, and social scientist who showed the way toward what economic science could be and how it need not take the form of NE. He was both a critic of NE and a scholar who developed new economic theory and perspectives. There is no doubt that he sought to develop an economics (behavioral economics) that was less narrow, rigid, intolerant, mechanical, separate, and individualistic than NE. He wanted an economics in which the concept of rationality was realistically linked to knowledge of other social science disciplines, especially psychological knowledge. He sought to improve human rationality in decision making and to replace the NE assumption of global, utility maximizing rationality. Perhaps because the time was not right, or because his inclinations were more toward reform of NE, or because his scientific contributions to economics were not considered sufficient, or because of his leadership qualities, he did not become the leader of a scientific revolution during his lifetime. If BE were to be recognized in the future as the superior paradigm poised to overthrow NE, theories and perspectives developed by Herbert Simon would presumably have to be very important elements of the new paradigm.

References

Augier, Mie and March, James G. 2002. "A Model Scholar: Herbert A. Simon (1916–2001)," *Journal of Economic Behavior and Organization*, 49, 1–17.

Berg, Nathan and Gigerenzer, Gerd. 2010. "As-If Behavioral Economics: Neoclassical Economics in Disguise?" *History of Economic Ideas*, 43(1), 133–165.

Gigerenzer, Gerd and Goldstein, Daniel G. 1996. "Reasoning the Fast and Frugal Way: Models of Bounded Rationality," *Psychological Review*, 103(4), 650–669.

Gigerenzer, Gerd and Selten, Reinhard. 2001. "Rethinking Rationality," in Gigerenzer, Gerd and Selten, Reinhard (eds) *Bounded Rationality: The Adaptive Toolbox.* Cambridge, MA: The MIT Press, 1–12.

Selten, Reinhard. 2001. "What Is Bounded Rationality?" in Gigerenzer, Gerd and Selten, Reinhard (eds) *Bounded Rationality: The Adaptive Toolbox.* Cambridge, MA: The MIT Press, 13–36.

Simon, Herbert A. 1955. "A Behavioral Model of Rational Choice," *Quarterly Journal of Economics*, 69, February, 99–118.

Simon, Herbert A. 1959. "Theories of Decision-Making in Economics and Behavioral Science," *American Economic Review*, 49(3), June, 253–283.

Simon, Herbert A. 1976. "From Substantive to Procedural Rationality," in Latsis, Spiro J. (ed) *Method and Appraisal in Economics.* Cambridge: Cambridge University Press, 129–148.

Simon, Herbert A. 1978. "Rationality as Process and as Product of Thought," *American Economic Review*, 68(2), May, 1–16.

Simon, Herbert A. 1983. *Reason in Human Affairs.* Stanford: Stanford University Press.

Simon, Herbert A. 1987. "Behavioral Economics," in Eatwell, John, Milgate, Murray and Newman, Peter (eds) *The New Palgrave: A Dictionary of Economics.* New York: Stockton Press, 221–225.

Simon, Herbert A. 1992. "Rational Decision-Making in Business Organizations," (Nobel Memorial Lecture December 8, 1977) in Lindbeck, Assar (ed) *Nobel Lectures: Economic Sciences 1969–1980.* London: World Scientific.

4 The basics of the psychological economics strand

Psychological economics: origins and orientations

As stated in Chapter 2, Daniel Kahneman and Amos Tversky are recognized as the founders of the psychological economics (PE) strand of behavioral economics (BE). To gain a full appreciation of PE, it is important to inquire into the roots of PE. PE's origins are in cognitive psychology. In essence, PE is the product of the application of cognitive psychology to the realm of economic decision making (Angner and Loewenstein 2007, p. 2). Given its origins, it is understandable that from the start PE was concerned largely with the cognitive aspects of decision making and very little with the non-cognitive aspects such as emotions, moods, and feelings. However, in later years, the non-cognitive aspects of decision making have assumed a greater importance in PE than was the case earlier. It is also notable that PE shares cognitive psychology's repudiation of the positivistic scientific methods of neoclassical economics (NE).

With regard to PE's origins, it is important to recognize the role of "behavioral decision research [BDR], which itself can be seen as a melding of ideas from economics and cognitive science" (Angner and Loewenstein 2007, p. 2).[1] BDR notably has made use of NE's rational choice theory. That theory has served as a research "target" that BDR researchers utilized when evaluating the rationality of people's decision making responses in research settings. Comparing the clear predictions of rational choice theory to people's actual behavior made it possible to better understand when and to what extent people's judgments and decisions were irrational. Note that in such comparisons merely random deviations from the rational norm are of little interest. The deviations of greatest interest are those that are systematic and predictable (p. 29).

In the 1970s, Kahneman and Tversky admirably brought BDR to the attention of economists (Angner and Loewenstein 2007, p. 30) and developed it in a way that was persuasive to many economists. Through these efforts, PE (which in the eyes of some researchers is the same as BE) grew out of BDR and gradually emerged as its own field (p. 37). According to Rabin (1996, p. 111), Kahneman and Tversky's success resulted from the fact that "they were able and willing to address economists in standard economic language and venues." Owing to its BDR origins, PE (the new BE) has been critical of NE's rational decision theory when it is used as a positive or descriptive theory, but it has been accepting of rational decision theory when it is used as a normative or prescriptive theory.

PE also reflects BDR in some other respects. "A central focus of behavioral decision researchers is to identify the common set of [human] cognitive skills, their benefits and limitations, and to explore how they produce observable behavior" (Angner and Loewenstein 2007, p. 29). Most important in this regard is the understanding that the capacity of humans' working memory is limited. Because of this humans frequently depart from optimal, rational behavior (Hastie and Dawes 2001, p. 10). Moreover, "diverse people in very different situations often think about their decisions in the same way. We have a common set of cognitive skills that are reflected in similar decision habits. But we also bring with us a common set of limitations on our thinking skills that can make our choices far from optimal" (p. 2).

As indicated in Chapter 2, PE's basic methods and assumptions do not represent a radical departure from those of NE (Rabin 2002, pp. 658–659). Nevertheless, "there are many assumptions that [NE] economists make about human nature that . . . [PE] research suggests are often importantly wrong. These include the assumptions that people . . . 1) have well-defined and stable preferences; 2) maximize their expected utility; 3) exponentially discount future well-being; [and] 4) are self-interested, narrowly defined . . ." (p. 660). According to Rabin, "the goal of PE is to investigate behaviorally grounded departures from . . . [NE] assumptions that seem economically relevant" (p. 660). This is important because NE methods emphasize mathematical precision and generality, and use simplified models of human mental processes, thereby omitting a great amount of psychological reality (p. 672). Accordingly, PE researchers believe that it is important to introduce psychological conceptions of human nature that may be less simple and general than NE assumptions but more accurately reflect how people think and behave.

Heuristics and biases

During the 1970s and 1980s, Kahneman and Tversky along with a number of their research collaborators identified quite a few human judgment and decision biases. Let's start with the three biases that are the subject of their very important 1974 *Science* article entitled "Judgment under Uncertainty: Heuristics and Biases." These three biases are availability, anchoring and adjustment, and representativeness. Because of these biases, humans regularly make systematic and predictable errors in their judgment and decision making in certain kinds of situations. In other words, humans are predictably irrational.

Heuristics are rules of thumb, involving simplifications of reality, that people use to make judgments. Because our lives are often busy and complicated, we do not have time to carefully think about and analyse all the different situations we encounter. Therefore, we use rules of thumb that are quick, useful, and simple (Thaler and Sunstein 2009, p. 22). Particular rules of thumb are used automatically in certain situations to make intuitive judgments and decisions. According to Kahneman and Tversky, these heuristics belong to the "human informal processing machinery that cannot be changed" (Heukelom 2014, p. 118). In other words, they are part of the "unchanging biological makeup of the individual."[2] A good heuristic can be used quickly and can enable close to optimal decision making. Nevertheless, these rules of thumb violate logical principles and contribute to errors in some situations (Camerer and Loewenstein 2004, p. 11). Thus, according to Kahnemen and Tversky, humans are imperfect statisticians, logicians, and optimizers of utility (Heukelom 2014, p. 118).

Availability

The availability bias relates to "situations in which people judge the frequency . . . or probability of an event by the ease with which instances . . . can be brought to mind" (Tversky and Kahneman 1974, p. 1127). What is the likelihood that we will be impacted by risky events such as a hurricane, flooding, a terrorist attack, an alligator attack, an earthquake, a homicide, and so on? Our estimates of the likelihood (or probability) of these events are often biased because our estimates are not the same as the true probabilities. Typically, we overestimate the probability of events that readily come to mind. "Thus vivid and easily . . . [remembered] causes of death . . . often receive inflated estimates of probability, and less-vivid causes . . . receive low estimates, even if they occur with a far greater frequency" (Thaler and Sunstein 2009, p. 25). Evidence supporting this is that "in the aftermath of an earthquake, purchases of new earthquake insurance policies rise sharply . . . [and] if floods have not occurred in the immediate past, people who live on floodplains are far less likely to purchase insurance" (p. 25). A related factor is salience. If you have seen a house burn down, your estimate of fire probability is probably greater than if you merely read about the house fire in your local newspaper. Imaginability is another factor related to bias. If you can easily and vividly imagine risks associated with an adventurous expedition, you are more likely to overestimate the probability of these risks (Tversky and Kahneman 1974, pp. 1127–1128). A slightly different but related bias is hindsight bias. People tend to over or under estimate the probability they attached to events that later happened. This can lead to Monday-morning quarterbacking. On the day after the football game, because your estimate of the probability of your team's quarterback throwing intercepted passes is much higher, but not necessarily less biased, you may believe you can see clearly what the quarterback should have done to avoid those interceptions (Camerer and Loewenstein 2004, p. 10).

Anchoring and adjustment

Another type of bias in judgment results from a process called anchoring and adjustment. This occurs when a person is asked to make a judgment or estimate about a matter in which the person has relatively little knowledge. In this process, the person starts from some initial value (the anchor) and adjusts this value upward or downward, attempting to come up with an estimate that is better than the anchor value. Bias occurs because the chosen adjustments are typically insufficient (Tversky and Kahneman 1974, pp. 1128–1130). To illustrate, suppose you are asked to guess/estimate the population of the city of Milwaukee, a city a couple of hours drive north of Chicago (Thaler and Sunstein 2009, p. 23). If you are a resident of Chicago and you know that Chicago's population is about three million, you probably also know that Milwaukee, while sizeable, is quite a bit smaller than Chicago. Using Chicago's population as your anchor, you might guesstimate Milwaukee's population to be one million. Now suppose you are a resident of Green Bay, Wisconsin, a city with one hundred thousand residents, and you know that Milwaukee is larger. Using the one hundred thousand population figure as your anchor, you adjust upward and might guesstimate Milwaukee's population at three hundred thousand. It turns out that Milwaukee's population is 580,000. In this example, both persons used their own city's population as the anchor and adjusted insufficiently in the right direction, resulting in biased estimates of Milwaukee's population. This indicates how people often rely on a somewhat relevant anchor when making estimates. There is evidence, though, that people can even be strongly influenced by arbitrary anchors. In an experiment with college students, Dan Ariely (2009, pp. 26–29) asked the students to write down the maximum amount they would be willing to pay for particular bottles of fine wine. Before making these wine judgments, the students were requested to write down the last two digits of their social security numbers on the page where they would write the amount they would be willing to pay. Ariely's analysis of the data from this experiment indicated surprisingly that the students' social security numbers did serve as anchors. "The students with the highest-ending social security digits (80 to 99) bid highest, while those with the lowest ending numbers (1 to 20) bid lowest" (p. 28). Interestingly, once the students had made their estimate for one bottle of a particular quality of wine, "their willingness to pay for other [qualities of wine] . . . was judged relative to that first price" (now an anchor) (p. 29). The upshot is that while "initial prices are largely 'arbitrary' and can be influenced by responses to random questions . . . once those prices are established [anchored] in our minds, they shape not only what we are willing to pay for an item, but also how much we are willing to pay for related products" (p. 30).

Representativeness

Representativeness is the third bias analysed in Tversky and Kahneman's (1974) article. This bias typically arises when people are asked probabilistic questions of the type: What is the probability that object (or event or process) A belongs to class B? (p. 1124). In answering this type of question, people typically rely on whether their stereotype of A seems to resemble or represent their image of B. Thus, when their stereotype of A highly resembles that of B, they judge the probability that A originates from B to be high, and vice versa (p. 1124). Consider this example: you are asked to consider a woman who is described as a "shy poetry lover." Is it more probable that she 1) studies Chinese literature or 2) studies business administration? Many people who rely on their stereotypes are likely to choose answer 1. This is because a shy poetry lover does not seem to resemble the stereotype associated with a business administration student (Kahneman 2011, p. 152). But answer 2 is a better answer. The population of business students is much, much larger than the population of Chinese literature students. So it is very likely that there are more shy poetry lovers in the business student population than in the population of students of Chinese literature. There is no doubt that using the stereotype, i.e., judging by representativeness, has some truth, and in some circumstances can be accurate. Nevertheless, judging probability using representativeness often leads to serious errors because it does not consider a number of factors that generally affect judgments of probability.[3] In the case above, it does not consider the respective sizes of the populations of business students and Chinese literature students (Tversky and Kahneman 1974, p. 1124).

Discussion

Each of the three heuristics (representativeness, availability, and anchoring and adjustment) discussed above consist of short-cut rules or processes that people typically use either to estimate probabilities or values or to select actions. For representativeness, the heuristic is to use the match of two stereotypes to judge the probability that item A belongs to class B. For availability, the heuristic is to use the ease with which an instance can be brought to mind to judge the relative probability of different events. For anchoring and adjustment, the heuristic is to use a prominent known value as a starting point in finding an estimate of a sought after value and then to adjust that value in a direction that seems to make sense. Each of these three heuristics or rules of thumb can serve as a simple, manageable, useful, quick method to make judgments or help make decisions. However, the use of each of them can cause people to make systematic, predictable, and sometimes severe errors. Due to these errors or biases, the judgments and choices made using these heuristics will deviate from the economically rational norms associated with NE. These errors occur not because people are not trying to make the best or optimal decision. The systematic deviations from optimality occur because of the way people make decisions, i.e., they use the heuristics discussed above and many others (Heukelom, 2014, pp. 116–118). It should be noted that Kahneman and Tversky do not find fault with NE's expected utility theory as a normative theory; they use the normative theory. They, however, disagree strongly with NE's positive or descriptive theory of judgment and choice (p. 127).

To fully understand heuristics and the resulting biases, it is important to make a distinction between two kinds of thinking. The first kind of thinking uses the Automatic System (also known as System

1). The second kind of thinking uses the Reflective System (also known as System 2). Automatic System thinking is intuitive, rapid, and instinctive, and it involves little effort or voluntary control. Using their automatic thinking, people often use their gut reactions to rapidly size up situations (Thaler and Sunstein 2009, pp. 19–21; Kahneman 2011, pp. 20–21). On the other hand, Reflective System thinking is deliberate, orderly, effortful, and self-conscious, and it requires self-control and attention (pp. 21–22). Much of the time, we operate in the automatic or intuitive mode; this system cannot be turned off (p. 25). It is when we are making judgments and choices in the intuitive, fast-thinking mode that we may automatically resort to the kinds of heuristics discussed above. But "the spontaneous search for an intuitive solution sometimes fails – neither an expert solution nor a heuristic answer comes to mind. In such cases we often find ourselves switching to a slower, more deliberate and effortful form of thinking" (p. 13). Such reflective thinking regarding a problem requires us to pay careful attention to it. This uses up part of our limited budget of attention, thereby making less attention available to deal with other problems (p. 23). Accordingly, people are typically reluctant to invest more attentive effort in problems and issues than is absolutely necessary (pp. 31, 40–41). It should be noted that while automatic, intuitive thinking is subject to the errors associated with the use of heuristics, this type of thinking can be accurate, especially when trained or practiced over considerable time (p. 4; Thaler and Sunstein 2009, p. 21).

If people have strong tendencies to be biased in their judgments and decisions, can they learn to eliminate or reduce these biases? And are people with much relevant experience and expertise able to avoid these errors? Research suggests a negative answer to both these questions. Unfortunately, learning does not seem to do much to eliminate or reduce these biases (Rabin 1998, p. 31). And experts are also not able to avoid these biases:

> The reliance on heuristics and prevalence of biases are not restricted to laymen. Experienced researchers are also prone to the same biases – when they think intuitively. For example, the tendency to [poorly] predict the outcome that best represents the data ... has been observed in the intuitive judgments of individuals who have had extensive training in statistics. Although the statistically sophisticated avoid elementary errors, ... their intuitive judgments are liable to similar fallacies in more intricate and less transparent problems. (Tversky and Kahneman 1974, p. 1130)

No doubt, most people have difficulties with statistical thinking. But there is another "puzzling limitation of our mind: our excessive confidence in what we believe we know and our apparent inability to acknowledge the full extent of our ignorance and the uncertainty of the world we live in" (Kahneman 2011, pp. 13–14). Laymen and experts alike are too reliant on (and overconfident in) their intuitive thinking (p. 45). Of course, it is possible that people can learn to recognize situations in which mistakes are likely and try harder to avoid these mistakes, especially in the presence of high stakes. But due to excessive confidence in their intuitions, people, regardless of their expertise, do too little learning and correcting of their errors.

Prospect theory

Introduction

After publishing their work on heuristics and biases (H&B), Kahneman and Tversky turned their attention to developing prospect theory (PT). The culmination of that work in the 1970s was their 1979 *Econometrica* article entitled "Prospect Theory: An Analysis of Decision Under Risk." PT is essentially an extended version of H&B that focuses largely on financial decisions involving risk (Heukelom 2014, p. 119). As in H&B, the people depicted in PT are hypothesized to rely on a set of heuristics in their decision making. In addition to this focus on the process of decision making, PT seeks to answer a key question: do decision makers consistently behave in accordance with the subjective expected utility theory of NE? Very similar to the H&B investigations, the findings of PT research are that when humans rely on a set of heuristics, the decision outcomes typically deviate from the rational norms of expected utility theory in a systematic and predictable way. In essence, this is because people lack the capacity to behave according to expected utility theory (p. 119). Note that although PT is to a great extent a cognitive psychology theory, it has been carefully constructed to appeal to economists (p. 120).

As in H&B, PT describes people as making decisions intuitively (Automatic System thinking) using rules of thumb (heuristics). The decision outcomes often involve errors or mistakes because individuals frequently have a biased perception of the probabilities and payoffs involved (Heukelom 2014, pp. 124–126). Individual decision makers are no doubt trying to make the best possible decisions, but they are busy and cannot take the time to think deeply and carefully about the complexities of the situations they face (Thaler and Sunstein 2009, p. 37). Thus, the goal of PT is to document and explain the systematic deviations of decision making from the rational norms of expected utility theory.

The empirical research of Kahneman and Tversky generally took place in labs where subjects were typically presented with financial outcomes and different probabilities and were asked to make a decision (Heukelom 2014, p. 121). The options faced by the lab decision makers often involved a risk of monetary loss and an opportunity for monetary gain. Would the subjects be willing (or not) to take the gamble in these relatively simple hypothetical scenarios? (Kahneman 2011, pp. 283–284).

To understand the contribution of PT, it is useful to start with the insights that Daniel Bernoulli developed back in 1738 (Kahneman 2011, pp. 272–275). His insight relates to a person's comparison of the value of two alternative monetary amounts, A and B, that this person might expect to receive. To compare the two amounts, it is first necessary to adjust these amounts so that they reflect the psychological value or desirability (utility) of the money involved. Second, the person must multiply the utility of A and B by the respective probabilities that the money amounts will be received. So in Bernoulli's view, what a person should compare are the expected values of the utility of A and B. Further, Bernoulli's theory assumes that it is the utility of a person's wealth that makes a person happy (p. 275). Therefore, to compare the happiness of two persons, Jack and Jill, it is necessary to consider not only the expected value of the received amount but also how the received amount would contribute to Jack and Jill's resulting wealth. Note that the utility values used by Bernoulli are the expected utilities of Jack and Jill's wealth. In this respect, according to PT, Bernoulli's analysis involves a serious error. "Bernoulli's theory assumes that the utility of . . . [a person's] wealth is what makes . . . [the person] more or less happy" (p. 275). PT corrects this assumption by explaining that the happiness one experiences from receipt of a monetary amount is determined by the change in the utility of their wealth relative to a reference point. Different people starting out with different amounts of wealth will place different values on the receipt of a given amount of money. Thus, PT has improved on conventional economic wisdom by defining the relevant decision outcomes as gains or losses in utility (psychological value), not as states of wealth (p. 279).

Key features of prospect theory

A key feature of PT analyses is that a person's evaluation of the results of gamble choices is relative to a neutral reference point. The reference point may refer to a starting point that could be an adaptation level, a level to which people have become adapted. Alternatively, the reference point could simply be the status quo; or perhaps it is an outcome that people feel entitled to. If the value of an outcome is higher than the reference point, choosing it produces a gain; if it is below the reference point, its choice produces a loss (Kahneman 2011, p. 282). PT focuses on these gains and losses, changes in wealth or welfare from some reference point. Stimuli such as brightness, loudness, and temperature, as well as non-sensory attributes (health, prestige, and wealth) are all perceived in relation to a reference point (Heukelom 2014, pp. 123–124). Note that gains and losses, particularly material payoffs with associated probabilities, are generally subjectively perceived, and thus, have perceived values only loosely correlated with objective measures of change.

Another common feature related to the outcomes of PT research is diminishing sensitivity (Kahneman 2011, pp. 282–283). This feature is akin to the economic principle of diminishing marginal utility. Diminishing sensitivity occurs when the extra psychological value of the extra gain (say in wealth, health, or nourishment) becomes smaller and smaller. Diminishing sensitivity also applies to losses as the extra losses in psychological value become smaller and smaller as extra losses in the good are incurred. Diminishing sensitivity can also apply to a phenomenon such as a light source (p. 283). When a little extra light is added to a dark room, it will have a relatively large effect. However, adding the same extra light to an already brightly illuminated room will have a relatively much smaller effect.

Loss aversion

An important aspect of people's behavior is how they value gains and losses. Most people hate losses and place a higher psychological value on them than they do on gains. Consider a relatively simple example.

You are offered a gamble on the toss of a coin.
If the coin shows tails, you lose $100.
If the coin shows heads, you win $150.
Is this gamble attractive? Would you accept it? (Kahneman 2011, p. 283)

Research indicates that for most people the prospect (or fear) of losing $100 is more intense than the hope of gaining $150. The typical person needs a gain of $200 to just balance the $100 loss (p. 284). This loss aversion tends to produce inertia; people are inclined to stay with the status quo rather than possibly incur a painful loss (Thaler and Sunstein 2009, pp. 33–34). The putting decisions of professional golfers provide a good example. A golfer might be in a position to make a relatively safe putt to attain par or could attempt a risky putt to attain a birdie (one stroke under par) but risk a bogey (one stroke over par). The evidence indicates that the fear of loss (bogey) has caused golfers more often and more successfully to putt for par despite the tournament rewards for birdies (Kahneman 2011, pp. 303–304). Other situations in which loss aversion can be an important influence include "investors who evaluate a start-up, lawyers who wonder whether to file a lawsuit, wartime generals who consider an offensive, and politicians who must decide whether to run for office" (p. 283). In general, "loss aversion is a powerful conservative force that favors minimal changes from the status quo in the lives of both institutions and individuals. This conservatism helps keep us stable in our neighborhood, our marriage, and our job; it is the gravitational force that holds our life together near the reference point" (p. 305).

In Kahneman and Tversky's (1979, p. 279) original article on PT, they drew a graph of the "value function." That graph of a hypothetical value function is shown in Figure 4.1 below. Psychological value is plotted on the vertical axis of the graph; positive values are located above the origin, and negative values are below. The horizontal axis measures gains to the right of the origin and losses to the left of the origin, which is a neutral reference point. To the right of the origin, the value function rises in a convex fashion; with rising gains, the corresponding increases in value are diminishing. This reflects diminishing sensitivity. To the left of the origin, the value function decreases in a concave fashion; with rising losses, the corresponding decreases in value are diminishing. This also reflects diminishing sensitivity. Also noteworthy is that the slope of the value curve changes abruptly at the reference point (origin). The slope of the curve indicates the value of the gains or losses. Because of loss aversion, the slope of the value function in the loss region is steeper or higher than its slope in the gain region. This is because for any given dollar amount of gain or loss, the value of the loss is greater than the value of the gain (loss aversion). In other words, for a person experiencing the same dollar amount of loss and gain, the loss is experienced as having a greater impact than the gain.

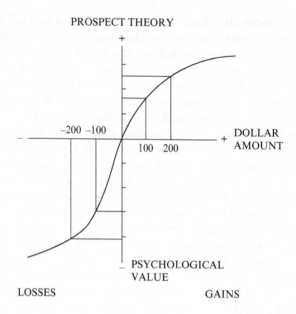

Figure 4.1   Prospect theory graph

Endowment effect

The endowment effect is another noteworthy behavioral regularity that from the standpoint of NE is not rational. What has been observed is that people consistently demand much more money to give up an object than they would be willing to pay to acquire it (Kahneman, Knetsch, and Thaler 1991). The endowment effect relates to people who possess an object and value it more than people not so endowed. Giving up the object is experienced as a loss, and because losses are valued more than gains (loss aversion), the possessors of the object insist on being paid an amount reflecting the pain associated with their loss, an amount that is substantially greater than they would pay initially to get the object. The classic example is the experiment in which half of the randomly selected subjects were given a decorated Cornell University coffee mug priced at $6 at the bookstore. They were then asked about the lowest price for which they would be willing to sell the mug. To obtain a mug, the other half of the subjects would have to make an offer to buy the mug using their own money. "The results were dramatic: The average selling price was about double the average buying price" (Kahneman 2011, p. 295). Apparently, the high price set by sellers indicates that they insisted on being compensated for the pain of giving up their mug (p. 296). Another group of subjects in the experiment called "choosers" were not given the mug, but could receive a sum of money for agreeing to allow ownership of the mug to be transferred to someone else. The money amounts acceptable to choosers were about half of the amount required by the sellers. From a strict economic perspective, this does not make sense. The only difference between the two situations is that the sellers are "giving up a mug they own whereas choosers are merely giving up the right to have a mug" (Camerer and Loewenstein 2004, p. 16). The different behaviors of sellers and choosers only makes sense when we contemplate the considerable reluctance of the mug owners to give up their endowment (p. 296). Similar experiments have replicated the endowment effect. Particularly interesting results have been found in the cases of 1) the professor who was reluctant to sell old wine bottles from his collection, 2) the Duke University students who were unwilling to sell tickets they had won to attend a Duke national championship basketball game, and 3) people who refuse to sell some of their cherished clutter (Ariely 2009, pp. 129–134). There is one significant exception to the endowment effect. This is the case where the good in question is held "for exchange" rather than "for use." If you are a professional trader of a good, you do not typically experience a loss when selling a good. It is also unlikely for you to experience a loss when you give up money to buy desired goods (Kahneman 2011, p. 294). The traded goods and the money are held for exchange not for use.

Status quo bias

As explained earlier, loss aversion is an important reason for people's preference for the status quo. People often do not want to change their situations because they believe the pain of the losses will substantially exceed the value of the gains. In other cases, the status quo bias is a matter of the power of inertia (Thaler and Sunstein 2009, p. 8). People simply have a strong tendency to stick with their current situations. Students usually sit in the same classroom seat every period, and people who choose retirement savings plans typically pick a plan and then never change it (p. 34). Another "cause of status quo bias is a lack of attention . . . [sometimes called] the 'yeah whatever' heuristic" (p. 35). For such reasons, people strongly tend to accept the default options on the consumer electronic devices they buy. This consumer acceptance of the default option might also be because the default seems to come "with an implicit endorsement from the default setter" (p. 35). Another more complicated situation that favors remaining at the status quo is the case of negotiations in which a settlement can only be reached when the different parties each accept a loss in exchange for a gain. Because the losses invariably cause more pain than the gains give pleasure, going beyond the status quo and reaching a mutually acceptable agreement is generally quite difficult (Kahneman 2011, pp. 304–305). A study of decision making related to two types of auto insurance in the states of New Jersey and Pennsylvania revealed an interesting status quo bias (Hershey et al. 1990). The authors "found that residents . . . [in both states] chose different insurance options from very similar sets of choices, based simply on which option was presented as the default one" (Weber and Dawes 2005, pp. 11–12; see also Kahneman, Knetsch, and Thaler 1991, p. 199).

Framing

In some cases, people make large, systematic, and predictable errors in decision problems simply because of how the problems are framed. As Tversky and Kahneman (1981, p. 453) point out, "it is often possible to frame a given decision problem in more than one way." Seemingly inconsequential changes in how a decision problem is stated can lead people to make different decisions, and not infrequently, less rational choices (p. 457). In other words, framing bias can occur when "a logically equivalent (but not transparently equivalent) statement of a problem" leads a decision maker to choose an inferior option (Rabin 1998, p. 36). Different frames may invoke different emotional reactions, and thus, different automatic (or System 1) thinking (Kahneman 2011, p. 88). For example, one frame might highlight monetary losses whereas another frame might draw attention to gains. Or the decision problem might involve living or dying outcomes resulting from medical treatments. Suppose you have a serious heart disease and your doctor recommends a major operation (Thaler and Sunstein 2009, p. 36). Your doctor might say, "Of one hundred patients who have this operation, ninety are alive after five years." Or suppose he/she instead says, "Of one hundred patients who have this operation, ten are dead after five years." If you are like most people, you would be a lot less likely to choose the operation if your doctor made the second statement. This is because the second statement highlights dying rather than living. Due to your emotional reaction to the thought of dying, your automatic system is more likely to lead you to reject the operation even though the content of the two doctor statements is the same. Another interesting example of framing involves the different prices that retail merchants have wanted to charge their cash and credit card customers (p. 36; Tversky and Kahneman 1981, p. 456). There has been significant resistance to the idea of credit card customers paying a surcharge (i.e., paying more than the cash customers). However, the resistance largely vanished when the situation was reframed as the credit card customers paying the normal or default price and the cash customers as receiving a discount. In such situations where framing is important, is it possible for people to make an extra mental effort and to switch to using their reflective (System 2) thinking in order to understand the frame and how it might bias their choice? Of course it is. But as Thaler and Sunstein (2009, p. 37) point out, "people tend to be somewhat mindless, passive decision makers" who are reluctant to engage their reflective thinking.

Mental accounting

Mental accounting refers to how people organize information relevant to the decisions they make. It has much to do with keeping track of where money is going and keeping spending under control (Kahneman and Tversky 2000, p. xiv; Thaler 1999, p. 184). Mental accounting has a similarity to financial accounting which deals with recording and summarizing business transactions, and which is governed by numerous codified rules and conventions. Unlike financial accounting, mental accounting does not have codified rules; it is only possible to learn about the rules of mental accounting by observing behavior and inferring them (p. 184). Almost all people use mental accounting, but in many cases they are not aware of it (Thaler and Sunstein 2009, p. 50). Mental accounting in a sense frames the decision situations that a person or household faces. That framing leads people to make different decisions than they would otherwise have made (Thaler 1999, p. 186). Using mental accounting, people lump some information together and segregate other information in ways "that often violate standard assumptions of economic theory" (Kahneman and Tversky 2000, p. xiv).

The procedures of mental accounting were developed to help people economize on time and thinking costs and deal with their self-control problems. No doubt these procedures do not work perfectly; sometimes they create other difficulties (Thaler 1999, pp. 202–203). A common self-control problem that many people experience is saving enough money for particular purposes. To deal with this, people typically create mental savings accounts earmarked for particular purposes such as education, retirement, medical problems, "rainy days," or even "fun." The idea of such accounts is to make money available for the designated purpose and to make us unwilling to spend the money in these accounts for other purposes. It is a kind of financial self-control (Kahneman 2011, pp. 342–343; Thaler and Sunstein 2009, pp. 51–52). Using such mental accounts violates standard economic theory that assumes money is fungible. When money is fungible, money can be used for any purpose. Economists traditionally point out that it is irrational for money to be designated only for certain types of expenditures (Thaler 1999, p. 185). Even if it is irrational from a strict economic standpoint, mental accounting matters because it is an important influence on people's choices and because it provides people a measure of self-control and manageability that is often emotionally satisfying. Despite these benefits, using mental accounting can lead to problematic situations such as when people have a need to spend money to deal with an urgent situation, but they cannot spend the money on hand because that money is tied up in particular mental accounts. As a result, these persons may be forced to borrow money at an interest rate substantially higher than the rate they are earning on their savings accounts.

Mental accounting also operates at the casino. Gamblers typically call money they have won "house money" and put this money in a different pocket from the money they came in with. These gamblers are usually more willing to gamble with and take higher risks with house money (Thaler and Sunstein 2009, pp. 50–51). Another example of mental accounting deals with investing in the stock market. Suppose you need money for an important purpose such as to pay:

> the costs of your daughter's wedding and will have to sell some stock. You remember the price at which you bought each stock and can identify it as a 'winner', currently worth more than you paid for it, or as a loser. Among the stocks you own, Blueberry Tiles is a winner; if you sell it today you will have achieved a gain of $5000. You hold an equal investment in Tiffany Motors, which is currently worth $5000 less than you paid for it. . . . Which are you more likely to sell? (Kahneman 2011, p. 344)

Suppose, as many typically do, you consider the two stocks to be in separate mental accounts. One account contains a successful investment; the other contains a loser. If you sell Blueberry Tiles and close this account, it will give you the pleasure of experiencing a win. If you sell Tiffany Motors, closing this account will make your experience a painful loss. This is why "finance research has documented a massive preference for selling winners rather than losers" (p. 344). While always selling winners is understandable from a psychological perspective, doing so is often not economically rational. "A rational agent would have a comprehensive view of the portfolio and sell the stock that is least likely to do well in the future, without considering whether it is a winner or a loser" (p. 344).

Discussion

By the early 1980s, Kahneman and Tversky with the help of a number of others such as Richard Thaler had developed the essential elements of PE known as heuristics and biases and prospect theory. Because of these contributions, it had become very clear that NE's expected utility theory was mistaken, at least as a descriptive theory. The research of Kahneman and Tversky clearly indicated that there were many reasons why expected utility theory was not tenable as a theory of how people make decisions or as a theory relating to decision outcomes. Note that Kahneman and Tversky did not argue with NE's normative view of rationality. By the 1980s, the heuristics and biases and prospect theory research was gaining recognition as the essential component in the huge task of mapping out the many ways in which human decision making deviates systematically and predictably from economic rationality. The PE research of Kahneman and Tversky was also extremely important in the process of integrating economics with cognitive psychology and providing the basis for many subsequent behavioral economic applications.

Because of PE's emphasis on understanding why humans are often less than fully rational, PE has been criticized by some economists for presenting an unfairly negative view of humans' rational capabilities. These critics have argued that, "if human beings can send people to the moon and return them safely, they cannot be that irrational" (Heukelom 2014, p. 125). Kahneman seems to have reflected on these criticisms. Recently, he has somewhat moderated his view, and he admits that he now "understands the marvels as well as the flaws of intuitive thought" (Kahneman 2011, p. 10). Relatedly, it is interesting that a number of behavioral economists have recently begun to explain about and advocate for a "behavioral economics for smart people", in which the focus is on gaining understanding about how people are more rational and capable than suggested by PE research but still considerably less rational than the economic man of NE (see Altman forthcoming).

It should be noted that "Kahneman and Tversky's approach differs in a ... fundamental way from ... [Herbert] Simon's" approach (Heukelom 2014, p. 127). Simon, unlike Kahneman and Tversky, "considered [NE] economics to have embarked on the wrong track entirely" (p. 127). Simon not only rejected the NE descriptive theory of decision making, but he was also a strong critic of NE's normative theory of decision making (p. 127).

In several very important respects, PE is arguably a better economic science than NE. First, NE's methods including individualism, mathematical formalization of assumptions, and sophisticated statistical/empirical analyses require "highly simplified and stylized models of human cognition, preferences, and behavior that in every instance omit a tremendous amount of psychological reality" (Rabin 2002, p. 672). This makes it necessary to ignore important facets of human nature. "Psychology, by contrast, does ... dig deeper into the details of human nature, and is not ... as obsessed with the mathematical precision, generality, and empirical implementability of its findings" (p. 672). Clearly, PE's methods and its integration of psychological realism with economics are an important improvement over NE.

It is noteworthy that the research methods used by Kahneman and Tversky in their early research work were quite different from those typically employed by economists and were an important reason for the success of their research. It is beyond the scope of this chapter to explain about their research methods in detail but it is interesting to consider a few features of their methods. First, their experiments were typically carried out in the traditional experimental settings of psychologists and were done with a relatively small number of subjects. Second, the experimental trials with individual subjects were relatively time intensive. And third, their laboratory experiments provided settings in which all the relevant variables could be monitored and controlled (Heukelom 2014, pp. 128–129). Another experimental method they used consisted of administering questionnaires with hypothetical questions completed by subjects who were mainly students (p. 129). "It is safe to say that without the method of hypothetical questions, they could not have developed heuristics and biases and prospect theory" (p. 130).

Although Kahneman and Tversky were psychologists, it is clear that they aspired to make a major contribution to economists' understanding of how people make choices. In this, they succeeded. But it is important to note that they were not attempting to become economists. "What they intended to do, was rather to shift the economics-psychology border in such a way that their work and economics would become part of the same behavioral science" (p. 127). Because Kahneman and Tversky accepted many of the scientific norms and methods of economists, including economic rationality as a norm, it does not seem correct to consider them to be the creators of a new paradigm. It is, however, quite clear that their work has been instrumental to the successful emergence of behavioral economics which in recent years has produced a significant change in how economics is practiced.

NOTES

1 BDR is sometimes called behavioral decision making (BDM).

2 Herbert Simon used the term, heuristic, in a different way than Kahneman and Tversky (Heukelom 2014, p. 117). In Simon's view, individuals and organizations choose heuristics to make decisions, and if they were to find a heuristic unsatisfactory, it would be adjusted (p. 117). In the view of Kahneman and Tversky, however, individuals cannot adjust their heuristics (p. 118).

3 Strictly speaking, using representativeness could mean that the decision 1) is insensitive to the prior probability of outcomes, 2) is insensitive to sample size, 3) is insensitive to predictability, 4) involves misconceptions of chance, 5) involves an illusion of validity, or 6) fails to consider regression to the mean (Tversky and Kahneman 1974, pp. 1124–1126).

References

Altman, Morris. Forthcoming. *Handbook of Behavioral Economics and Smart Decision-Making: Rational Decision-Making Within the Bounds of Reason.* Cheltenham, UK and Northampton, MA: Edward Elgar Publishing.

Angner, Erik and Loewenstein, George. 2012. "Behavioral Economics" (January 14, 2007), in Uskali Maki (ed) *Handbook of the Philosophy of Science: Philosophy of Economics*, Amsterdam: Elsevier, 641–690. Available at SSRN.

Ariely, Dan. 2009. *Predictably Irrational: The Hidden Forces That Shape Our Decisions.* Revised edition. New York: HarperCollins.

Camerer, Colin F. and Loewenstein, George. 2004. "Behavioral Economics: Past, Present, Future," in Camerer, Colin F., Loewenstein, George and Rabin, Matthew (eds) *Advances in Behavioral Economics.* New York: Princeton University Press, 3–51.

Hastie, Reid and Dawes, Robyn. 2001. *Rational Choice in an Uncertain World: The Psychology of Judgment and Decision Making.* Thousand Oaks: Sage Publications.

Hershey, John, Johnson, Eric, Meszaros, Jacqueline and Robinson, Matthew. 1990. "What Is the Right to Sue Worth?" Wharton School, University of Pennsylvania, June.

Heukelom, Floris. 2014. *Behavioral Economics: A History.* New York: Cambridge University Press.

Kahneman, Daniel. 2011. *Thinking Fast and Slow*. New York: Farrar, Strauss, and Giroux.

Kahneman, Daniel and Tversky, Amos. 1979. "Prospect Theory: An Analysis of Decision Under Risk," *Econometrica*, 47(2), March, 263–291.

Kahneman, Daniel and Tversky, Amos. 2000. *Choices, Values, and Frames*. Cambridge: Cambridge University Press.

Kahneman, Daniel, Knetsch, Jack L. and Thaler, Richard H. 1991. "The Endowment Effect, Loss Aversion, and Status Quo Bias," *Journal of Economic Perspectives*, 5(1), Winter, 193–206.

Rabin, Matthew. 1996. "Daniel Kahneman and Amos Tversky," in Samuels, Warren J. (ed) *American Economists of the Late Twentieth Century*. Cheltenham UK, and Brookfield, VT: Edward Elgar Publishing Ltd, 111–137.

Rabin, Matthew. 1998. "Psychology and Economics," *Journal of Economic Literature*, 36(1), March, 11–46.

Rabin, Matthew. 2002. "A Perspective on Psychology and Economics," *European Economic Review*, 46, 657–685.

Thaler, Richard H. 1999. "Mental Accounting Matters," *Journal of Behavioral Decision Making*, 12(3), 183–206.

Thaler, Richard H. and Sunstein, Cass R. 2009. *Nudge: Improving Decisions About Health, Wealth, and Happiness*. Revised. New York, Penguin Books.

Tversky, Amos and Kahneman, Daniel. 1974. "Judgment under Uncertainty: Heuristics and Biases," *Science*, 185(4157), September 27, 1124–1131.

Tversky, Amos and Kahneman, Daniel. 1981. "The Framing of Decisions and the Psychology of Choice," *Science*, 211(4481), January 30, 453–458.

Weber, Roberto and Dawes, Robyn. 2005. "Behavioral Economics," in Smelser, Neil J. and Swedberg, Richard (eds) *The Handbook of Economic Sociology*, 2nd Edition Princeton: Princeton University Press, 90–108.

5 Psychological economics: important further developments

This chapter deals with a number of important developments in the psychological economics area. This chapter's four main sections are each concerned with how an important neoclassical economics (NE) behavioral assumption is flawed and how research efforts by behavioral economists have led to greater accuracy and realism in understanding human behavior.

The effect of emotions on judgment and decision making

As indicated in Chapter 2, neoclassical economists conceive of decision making as a cognitive process in which decision makers focus on the value of alternative actions in order to determine which action is optimal and should be chosen. NE decision makers are assumed to make their decisions entirely in a dispassionate manner. In Kahneman and Tversky's early decision theory research on heuristics, biases, and prospect theory, they also essentially conceive of decision making as a cognitive process (Loewenstien and Lerner 2003, p. 619). Where the psychological economics (PE) of Kahneman and Tversky differs from NE with respect to decision making is that PE identifies and explains about the "cognitive errors that people make when they judge the likelihood of future consequences" (p. 619; Angner and Loewenstein 2007, pp. 50–51). In recent decades, PE researchers, most notably George Loewenstein, have led the way in explaining how non-cognitive factors, such as emotions, are a very important influence on judgment and decision making. In Loewenstein's view, emotions, typically ones "experienced at the time of decision making, . . . often propel [people's] behavior in directions that are different from that dictated by a [dispassionate] weighing of the long-term costs and benefits of disparate actions" (Loewenstein 2000, p. 426). So understanding humans' emotions is certainly essential to understanding human decision making. But it should be noted that understanding human emotions is also essential to understanding many other aspects of human behavior because without emotional content, human behavior, even if clever and smart, would be detached from what gives life its richness.

To understand how emotions influence economic decision making, a good place to start is with Loewenstein's (2000, p. 426) theory concerning visceral factors. "Visceral factors refer to a wide range of negative emotions (e.g., anger, fear), drive states (e.g., hunger, thirst, sexual desire), and feeling states (e.g., pain) that grab people's attention and motivate them to engage in specific behaviors." Visceral factors are "affected by changing internal body states" and "can alter people's desires rapidly" (p. 426). Visceral factors have often been considered to be destructive forces, but they are also basic factors that a person needs to maintain the quality of his/her daily functioning (pp. 426–427). Contrary to traditional views on emotions, the influences of visceral factors are systematic and highly predictable. In Loewenstein's model (p. 427), the utility or satisfaction (u) that an individual receives from a consumption activity (c) is determined by the amount of his/her consumption and his/her corresponding visceral state (s). The mathematical formulation is: $u = f(c, s)$.

This means that the utility a person experiences from a specific kind of consumption will depend on the amount of that consumption and how the particular consumption activity and visceral factor are related (pp. 427–428). For instance, when a person is deprived of a certain type of consumption activity, this individual is likely to experience very strong emotion (visceral factor) and consequently will feel progressively worse. Therefore, at some point, the extra satisfaction this individual will be able to get from an additional amount of the consumption good/ activity will become greater and greater. In the case of food, continuing deprivation leads to increasingly strong hunger that causes an individual to intensify his/her preoccupation with obtaining food and lessens his/ her attention to other aspects of life. In the case of cocaine, an addict who is deprived of cocaine will experience very strong craving. As a consequence, all of the addicts' thoughts and attention will be focused on obtaining cocaine, and attention to all other things such as nourishment, sleep, loved ones, responsibility, and so on will vanish (p. 428). This is why "visceral factors often drive people to behave in ways that they view as contrary to their own self-interest" (p. 428).

To fully understand the influence of visceral factors on decision making, it is important to point out that the effect of these factors depends on their intensity level. At low levels of intensity, visceral factors have very little if any negative impact on the quality of a person's decision making (Loewenstein 1996, p. 273). With increases in the intensity of visceral factors, however, individuals' decision making becomes more and more adversely affected. At intermediate levels of intensity, decision makers are often acting impulsively and struggling with their efforts at self-control (p. 273). "At even greater levels of intensity, visceral factors can be so powerful as to virtually preclude decision making" in any meaningful sense (p. 273).

Let's further consider the effect of visceral factors at an intermediate level of intensity, i.e., in situations where these factors are an important influence on behavior but are not overwhelming. If an individual in such circumstances is attempting to decide in a careful, deliberative manner, visceral factors can override such deliberations (Loewenstein 2000, p. 428). In these situations, people often know that they are not acting in their own self-interest. They appreciate that there is a split between what they feel compelled to do and what they feel is best for them to do.

To fully understand a decision maker's behavior, it is important to know whether the person is in a "cold" state (i.e., not hungry, angry, in pain, etc.) or a "hot" state (i.e., craving, angry, jealous, sad, etc.).

> When in a 'cold' state . . ., it is difficult to imagine what it would feel like to be in a 'hot' state . . . or to imagine how one might behave in such a state. Likewise, when in a 'hot' state people have difficulty imagining themselves in a cold state and thus miscalculate the speed with which such a state will dissipate. Research has empirically demonstrated these 'hot-cold empathy gaps' (the misjudgments that occur between different visceral states). (Loewenstein 2000 p. 428)

People who are aware of the deleterious influence that their visceral factors might have may attempt to resist their future impact. Typically, however, this does not work, because people in cold states underestimate the influence of their future hot states.

Two general categories of behavior provide particularly interesting and important examples of the operation of visceral factors. These are bargaining behavior and intertemporal choice. In the case of bargaining behavior, people's anger toward those they are negotiating with can cause an individual negotiator to act contrary to his/her own and other negotiators' interests (Loewenstein 2000):

In the classical pattern of all visceral factors, angry negotiators become obsessed with causing pain to the other side, impatient to impose that pain (and relatively indifferent to the long-term consequences of doing so), and selfish (i.e., unconcerned about collateral damage to other parties). (p. 430)

The second area of special relevance to visceral factors is the case of otherwise normal people who are led to behave in ways that indicate extreme undervaluing (or discounting) of the future:

In the grip of 'road rage', suburban mothers in Alabama shoot each other over a trivial misunderstanding; politicians and business leaders become entangled in sex scandals that destroy their careers; people who have everything to gain from an attractive appearance fail to adhere to their diets. (p. 430)

Ariely and Loewenstein's (2006) article reports on an interesting and controversial study of emotions in decision making. It is an empirical study of the effect of sexual arousal on sexual judgment and decision making. The study's findings are generally supportive of the explanations above regarding the effect of emotions on decision making. The subjects of the study were male college students, some of whom were highly sexually aroused by erotic photographs and self-stimulation; the others (the control group) were in a neutral state. All these students were asked to "1) indicate how appealing they find a wide range of sexual stimuli and activities, 2) report their willingness to engage in morally questionable behavior in order to obtain sexual gratification, and 3) describe their willingness to engage in unsafe sex when sexually aroused" (p. 87). The results on the attractiveness of the listed activities indicate, not surprisingly, that these activities become much more sexually charged and attractive to the aroused students compared to the unaroused ones (p. 95). Arousal also "influences the intensity of motivation to have sex relative to other goals" (p. 95). And arousal decreases "the relative importance of other considerations such as behaving ethically toward a potential sexual partner" (p. 95). In general, the study's results indicate that for the aroused subjects, "goals other than sexual fulfillment become eclipsed by the motivation to have sex" (p. 95). The study's results clearly indicate that the influence of strong sexual emotion has a very significant effect on sexual decision making and judgment. Another interesting finding is the existence of a "hot–cold empathy gap", as the subjects who were unaroused failed to appreciate the magnitude of the influence that their sexual arousal would have on their judgment and decision making.

Paul Slovic and his collaborators have developed another way to under-stand how human emotions influence decision making. They have used the affect heuristic concept that has a clear link to Kahneman and Tversky's heuristics research. In Slovic's research, affect refers to a specific quality of goodness or badness that we experience due to our feelings about something we are evaluating or deciding about. In other words, affect refers to our emotional experience that has become attached to something that has our attention (Slovic et al. 2002, p. 397). We experience this affective response rapidly and automatically. When we rely on affect in our decision making and judgment, we are using the affect heuristic to some degree as a substitute for or a comple-ment to careful cognitive, analytical, deliberative processes. People use the affect heuristic, for example, when choosing the things we buy because reliance on affect is a quicker, easier, and perhaps more effi-cient way to make a purchase decision given the complex, uncertain situations we often face in the marketplace (p. 398). It should be noted that affect often involves subtle feelings of which people may be una-ware, and these feelings are often conditioned by our past experiences (pp. 398–401). Thus, people may "base their judgments of an activity or technology not only on what they *think* about it but also on what they *feel* about it. If they like an activity, they are moved to judge the risks as low and the benefits as high; if they dislike it, they tend to judge the opposite – high risk and low benefit" (pp. 410–411).

Although reliance on the affect heuristic can be useful and efficient, it can also deceive decision makers. The human experiential system has its limitations, and our affective reactions can be manipulated by people who wish to control our behaviors (p. 416). One example of the latter is how advertising, for example cigarette advertising, can evoke positive affect and depress our perceptions of risk (p. 417). Thus, the affect heuristic can be "wondrous in its speed, and subtlety, and sophistication, and its ability to 'lubricate reason' [but] frightening in its dependency upon context and experience, allowing us to be led astray or manipulated . . . silently and invisibly" (pp. 419–420).

To conclude, because people's purely cognitive assessments of situa-tions often greatly diverge from the assessments they make when they are influenced by emotion, it is essential that economists incorporate emotions into their theories of decision making. Emotions are at the heart of many people's self-control problems such as those related to hunger and dieting, sadness and impulsive suicide, anger and violence, sexual desire and sex crimes, fear and panic, and so on (Loewenstein

2000, p. 430). Unless we consider emotion, it is difficult to understand how people can behave self-destructively in "the heat of the moment." Further, it is becoming more and more clear that "many biases that had earlier been viewed in cognitive terms ... may in fact reflect the influence [of emotions]" (Angner and Loewenstein 2007, p. 51). And it is important to note that "important economic decisions such as major purchases often evoke powerful emotions" (Rick and Loewenstein 2008, p. 150). Neoclassical economists have traditionally left emotions out of their analyses because they believed such influences were transient and unimportant (Loewenstein 2000, p. 431). Fortunately, behavioral economists do not share the latter view, and they are learning to incorporate emotions in their analyses of judgment and decision making in a variety of ways (p. 431).

Self-interest and social preferences

In explaining the difference between NE and BE, the emphasis heretofore has been on comparing the rationality of the economic actors in NE (econs) to the frequent lack of rationality of the economic actors in PE (humans). However, there is another important difference between econs and humans; this relates to self-interest motivation. In contrast to econs who only pursue their self-interests, humans (in addition to being boundedly rational) are boundedly self-interested or "boundedly selfish" (Mullainathan and Thaler 2000, p. 5). What this means is that humans, unlike econs who care only about their own well-being, are motivated to care about the well-being of others and to be concerned for others' outcomes (Rabin 2002, p. 661). Such behavior is altruistic in the sense that humans are willing to sacrifice their own well-being for the sake of others. People are often altruistic in a general way, caring about all others' well-being, and sometimes they are altruistic in a manner targeted at selected others such as family members and friends (p. 665). Also in contrast to self-interested econs, "people care about the fairness and equity of the distribution of resources ... [and] care about intentions and motives, and want to reciprocate the good or bad behavior of others" (p. 665).

Behavioral economists have extensively investigated whether their behavioral suppositions concerning self-interest are true. One important strand of research involves the use of laboratory experiments. The most notable of these is the ultimatum game that was first developed by Werner Guth and colleagues in the early 1980s (Guth et al. 1982).

The ultimatum game is relatively simple. A sum of money, say $100, is allotted to two players. The first player, the Proposer, offers part of the money, X, to the second player, the Responder. Suppose X is $20. The Responder can keep that amount; consequently the Proposer can keep the remainder, 100-X or $80. Alternatively, the Responder can reject the Proposer's offer in which case both players receive nothing. Note that the players are anonymous and will never see each other again. If the Responder is an econ and is purely self-interested, she will accept any positive amount, even 10 cents or 1 cent. After all, if she does not accept this small amount, she will wind up with nothing. From a pure self-interest standpoint, it is better to have one cent than zero. The Proposer, on the other hand, is in a sense making an ultimatum offer. He is saying: here is my best offer, take it or leave it.

It turns out that the behavior of responders in these ultimatum games differs dramatically from the NE prediction of pure self-interested behavior. "In studies in more than 20 countries, the vast majority of proposers offer between a third and a half of the total, and responders reject offers of less than a fifth of the total about half of the time" (Camerer and Loewenstein 2004, p. 27). Why do responders reject offers that it is in their self-interest to accept? Consider a responder who is offered $8 out of $100 by the proposer. According to Rabin (2002, pp. 667–668), it is not difficult to understand what typically happens. The responder is willing to "sacrifice $8 to punish a jerk who wants to split $100 $92/$8 rather than $50/$50 (or at least $60/$40)." Such responders are consciously rejecting unfair offers and are taking revenge. They are not simply self-interested; they have a "taste for fairness and retaliation."

Behavioral economists have marshalled a great amount of other kinds of evidence indicating that humans care about others, not just themselves. It makes sense that if people cared only about themselves, they would always free ride, i.e., they would never voluntarily pay for or contribute to the cost of public goods. A public good is one that everyone can consume without diminishing the consumption of anyone else, and it is impossible to exclude anyone from consuming it. A fireworks display is a good example. There is a "social dilemma" involved in these public goods situations because although everyone has an incentive to free ride, everyone would be better off if no one did any free riding (Chaudhuri 2009, pp. 125–128). "In experiments that create social dilemmas in the laboratory, groups typically contribute 40 to 60 per cent of their stake to a public good. Thereby, they achieve a better outcome than they would if they all contributed the selfish, rational zero" (Thaler 1996, pp. 234–235). People are also observed to cooperate in many contentious interactions with others in which offering to cooperate with others might be disadvantageous to them. Behavioral economists have conducted many lab experiments to understand these kinds of behavior. What they find is "what we observe in life: many people donate to charity and public radio, clean up campgrounds, and conserve water in a drought. Yes there is lots of free riding, and it causes significant problems, but life would be much worse if people were as uncooperative as [NE] economic theory predicts" (p. 235).

Consider consumer transactions with businesses from a NE perspective. Sellers of the goods and services attempt to maximize their profit, and individual buyers attempt to maximize their satisfactions (or utility), both pursuing their respective self-interests without regard to ethical or moral considerations. In contrast to this perspective, behavioral economists have found that fairness is a major non-self-interest consideration in such transactions. To illustrate, let's start with an example deriving from the research of Kahneman, Knetsch, and Thaler (1986). They posed the following question to subjects in a telephone poll (Thaler 2015, p. 127–128; Chaudhuri 2009, p. 71–72). "A hardware store has been selling snow shovels for $15. The morning after a large snowstorm, the store raises the price to $20." Respondents were asked to rate the action as either acceptable or unfair. The responses were: 1) Acceptable 18% and 2) Unfair 82%.

Some people, especially individuals who have studied economics or business, may find it surprising that 82 percent of the respondents considered the price increase to be unfair. This is because from the standpoint of standard economics, raising the price makes sense. Assuming there is a fixed supply of shovels, the higher price will assure that the snow shovels wind up being owned by those who place the highest value on them. But from the standpoint of societal fairness norms that many people strongly hold, raising the price is clearly unacceptable and unfair. In contrast to neoclassical economists, behavioral economists recognize the importance that fairness norms play in understanding and constraining economic transactions.

Consider a few other examples of transactions in which the issue of fairness arises. On February 11, 2012, Whitney Houston, a very popular singer died suddenly. "It was to be expected that there would be a spike in the demand for her recordings, now largely sold online at sites such as iTunes" (Thaler 2015, p. 135). Less than a day after her death, the price of her 1997 album increased by 60 percent and the price of another album later increased by 25 percent. Does that violate the fairness norm? Suppose a country permits a free market in human organs such as kidneys. Then there is a possibility that a rich person who needs a kidney will pay a poor person to donate one (p. 130). Is that fair? Another interesting case involved the Coca-Cola company. At one point Coke's CEO proposed using vending machines that would change the price of a bottle of Coke according to environmental conditions such as the current temperature (pp. 134–135). If that happened, the price of Coke presumably would rise when people are hot and thirsty. Is that fair? When companies act unfairly or greedily, they may well be punished by their customers (assuming such companies' competitors do not follow their example). So taking a business action that is likely to be perceived as opportunistic and unfair can be a risky and unwise proposition (p. 136). Given the likely reactions of consumers, it would be wise for businesses to avoid a reputation for behaving unfairly (Chaudhuri 2009, p. 77). It is important to note that what is considered fair or unfair varies considerably across cultures. Also, it is noteworthy that fairness of procedures can matter as much as fairness of outcomes (p. 81). The upshot of the above is that humans, in contrast with econs, like to act fairly and be treated fairly, but will strike back if others treat them unfairly.

The foregoing has expressed the view that people are not motivated solely by their self-interests and has pointed out that there is a great deal of behavioral evidence supporting this. But, you might ask, what does brain science have to say about this? The starting point for understanding the fundamental types of human motivation is Paul MacLean's (1990) research on brain physiology. He conceived of the human brain as having three interconnected modular levels. The first module, the earliest in evolutionary terms, is the innermost core of the brain, the reptilian complex, which governs fundamental physiological operations and is concerned with self-preservation (Tomer 2012, p. 78). It is associated with self-interest motivation. The second part, the paleo-mammalian brain, is located on top of the reptilian brain. It provides for the distinctively mammalian features of humans such as maternal care, parental responsibility, family life, and social bonding. This part of the brain is associated with caring, other interest, and empathic motivation. The third module is the neo-mammalian brain or neocortex that envelops the other two brains. This part of the brain provides the human capacities for problem solving, learning, memory, language, thinking, and related functions. According to MacLean, the neocortex is involved in determining how the two strong core motivations, empathy deriving from the paleomammalian brain and self-interest deriving from the reptilian brain, are interrelated and expressed.

Based on the brain physiology research of MacLean, Gerald Cory (1999) developed a model known as dual motive theory (DMT) that explains how the two core human motivations tend to be balanced. In his view, it is the executive functioning of the brain's neocortex that attempts to bring about a balance between the self-interest and empathy motivations that not infrequently are in conflict with each other (Tomer 2012, pp. 78–79). Based on this understanding of brain physiology, it is quite clear that humans are not solely self-interested. In Tomer's (2012) revised DMT model, an individual's empathic capacity and functioning are determined not just by his/her genetically determined brain physiology but also by brain changes that happen as a consequence of an individual's unique path through life. In the revised DMT model, people still have two dominant motivations (ego and empathy), but the strength and character of an individual's empathic motivation depends very much on the individual's life experience and especially on whether the individual has made efforts to develop his/her empathic capacity. Further, according to Lynne et al. (2015), while the two core human motivations may be directly in conflict, generally the self-interest motive is primal, and a person's empathic capacity plays a restraining or conditioning role with respect to self-interest. That is, humans temper, restrain, and condition their self-interest motivation.

With the help of behavioral economics (BE) research in recent decades, we have come a long way from 1881 when Edgeworth asserted that "the first principle of Economics is that every agent is actuated only by self-interest" (as quoted in Sen 1977, p. 317). These days it is important to strive for realism and that means "economists should move away from the presumption that people are solely self-interested" (Rabin 1998, p. 16). Now "among experimentalists – and others paying attention to the evidence – the debate over whether there are systematic, non-negligible departures from self-interest is over" (Rabin 2002, p. 666). But, it is important to note that this "rejection of egoism as a description of motivation does not, therefore, imply the acceptance of some universalized morality as the basis of actual behavior. Nor does it make human beings excessively noble" (Sen 1977, p. 344). Humans are not "essentially kind and cooperative – altruistic – across the board" (Chaudhuri 2009, p. 8). Humans for the most part are conditional cooperators whose behavior often depends on what others are doing. Although humans are not saints, the good news, as Sen has pointed out, is that humans are not "rational fools ... blindly following only material self-interest" (Thaler 2015, p. 145).

Self-control

The third of the three key assumptions on which NE is built is self-control (Thaler 1996, p. 227). It is one thing to select an optimal or at least a good enough plan. It is, however, necessary to have considerable self-control in order to actually follow the plan. In a great many cases, humans lack the self-control necessary to do what they desire or intend to do. As Kahneman (2011, pp. 41–43) explains, self-control is a form of mental work; it requires attention and effort, and it can be tiring. In light of all the other things in life that require cognitive effort, people often do not have enough cognitive energy to exercise the degree of self-control necessary in order to accomplish the things that are important to them. So, too often we cannot get ourselves to do what we want to do or what we know we should do. One type of lack of self-control is procrastination. This is when we put off until "tomorrow" what we should do today (Ariely 2009, pp. 109–126). Therefore, our actions fall short of what our plans require. For example, we do not do enough today to exercise, diet, meet deadlines, follow important preventive health care, refrain from gambling, save for retirement or other important purposes, and so on. In many cases, we procrastinate because we succumb to the temptations of immediate gratification (pp. 110–111).[1] It is, of course, not uncommon that people recognize their self-control problems and make efforts to solve them. For example, people use alarm clocks, put money in Christmas clubs in order to have sufficient funds to buy Christmas presents, use budgeting and other forms of mental accounting, make lists of things to do, precommit to specific activities, and use a variety of other self-control strategies. All such things can help, but humans' self-control efforts nevertheless typically fall short, and thus, we fail to do all that we intend to do.

Summing-up on the three key assumptions

"Neoclassical economics is built on three assumptions: rationality, self-interest, and self-control" (Thaler 1996, p. 227). How does this compare with BE? To put it bluntly, behavioral economists have learned that "humans are dumber, nicer, and weaker than" econs (p. 227). In other words, BE research has found that humans are less rational, less self-interested, and less capable of self-control than the economic agents depicted in NE. It should be noted that the NE model "works best for simple, repeated tasks, and worst for complex infrequent tasks" (p. 235). It follows that "the most important life decisions: human capital formation, marriage, saving for retirement, job search, home purchase, etc. are all both difficult and rare, the worst case scenario for [NE]" (p. 235). The upshot according to Thaler (p. 235) is that "the assumptions of unbounded rationality, unbounded willpower [or self-control], and unbounded selfishness are convenient. They make [mathematical] models easy. But they are bad economics."

Time preference and choice

Another area where behavioral economists have arguably made a strong contribution is in analysing choice situations in which it is necessary for people to compare costs and benefits received in the future with those received in the present. Do people who make such comparisons count future costs and benefits the same as those in the present? Most people, including economists, believe that people place a higher value on current amounts. This is a reasonable thing to do. Because they count future values less, they are in a sense discounting future values. Simply put, people discount future values because they like to receive pleasant things soon and to delay unpleasant things. The NE view concerning how to deal with these intertemporal concerns derives from Paul Samuelson's writings in the late 1930s. He formulated "the standard economic model of intertemporal choice, the discounted utility [DU] model" (Thaler 2015, p. 89). According to this model, people apply increasingly large discounts (smaller and smaller discount factors (DF)) to values further and further in the future. In the DU model, the DF for year t equals $(1/1+r)^t$ where r is the discount rate. Thus, for year 2, the DF equals $(1/1+r)^2$. Note that the discount rate used in such calculations is considered to be close to the discount rate (or interest rate) used in financial markets and that the DF is a fraction less than one and more than zero (Weber and Dawes 2005, p. 8). Note also that the value of r can be considered a reflection of how impatient a person is to receive his/her future rewards. An important qualitative feature of the DU model is that it implies that people are time consistent, i.e., they are consistent about how much discounting is done for values between two time periods, regardless of how far from the present these values are (Rabin 1998, p. 38). A virtue of the DU model is that it captures the fact that people have a taste for immediate gratification and accordingly tend to procrastinate on tasks such as cleaning their house, tasks that involve immediate costs and delayed rewards. Note also that the DU model is consistent with the NE view that people attempt to maximize the present value of the future streams of utility from their experiences.

What behavioral economists have found is that the evidence regarding people's time preferences does not support the DU model. People's time preferences are not consistent over time:

> The behavioral evidence ... overwhelmingly and incontrovertibly shows that people exhibit *present-biased preferences*. [This means that] a person discounts near-term incremental delays in well-being more severely than she discounts distant-future incremental delays. [In other words] we are more averse to delaying today's gratification until tomorrow than we are averse to delaying the same gratification from [say] 90 days to 91 days from now. (Rabin 2002, p. 668)

Thus, people who are contemplating the rewards they expect to receive tomorrow feel a particularly urgent anticipation regarding the expected reward, an urgency that is not felt when they are contemplating receiving the reward in 90 days. This indicates that people tend to be very impatient and shortsighted with respect to valued outcomes that are expected very soon but are generally relatively patient or farsighted when pondering outcomes that are expected far in the future (Camerer and Loewenstein 2004, p. 23). The DU model does not capture this time inconsistency. But behavioral economists have found a model that captures very well people's behavior with respect to time. That model is the quasi-hyperbolic function. This function "is basically standard exponential time discounting plus an immediacy effect: a person discounts delays in gratification equally at all moments except the current one – caring differently about well-being now vs. later" (pp. 23–24). For a numerical example of hyperbolic discounting and how it can lead to time inconsistency, see Angner (2012, pp. 158–162). Another type of behavioral model relating to time preference is worthy of note. It has incorporated the idea that a person seems to have within him or herself two decision makers. One decision maker is farsighted and self-controlled; the other is impulsive and myopic, and thus, very focused on the present moment without regard for future consequences (Weber and Dawes 2005, p. 10). The key question here is the degree to which the rational farsighted aspect of a person will prevail. If the farsighted planner does prevail, the person may adopt surprisingly restrictive self-control measures that limit his or her future behavior.

Conclusion

As this chapter has explained, humans are less rational, less self-interested, and less self-controlled than the econs of NE. The first section of the chapter has explained how in the presence of emotion, especially strong negative emotion, it is not uncommon for people's judgments to be biased and their decisions to be irrational. The second section has explained how people are not solely self-interested or selfish; people's actions often reflect their caring and concern for others. The third section has explained how in many situations people lack the self-control that is necessary for them to do what they intend to do. And the fourth section has explained that with respect to time, people do not behave as consistently and rationally as NE theory indicates. Therefore, the overall conclusion is, not surprisingly, that people generally behave like humans, not the econs of NE. Fortunately, as this chapter explains, BE research is making a lot of progress both in understanding that NE is not realistic economics and also in gaining a greater, more realistic understanding of the economic behavior of humans.

NOTE

1 "Willpower is most relevant when decisions and rewards are separated in time implying that *delay of gratification* is necessary" (Thaler 1996, 235).

References

Angner, Erik. 2012. *A Course in Behavioral Economics*. New York: Palgrave Macmillan.

Angner, Erik and Loewenstein, George. 2012. "Behavioral Economics" (January 14, 2007), in Maki, Uskali (ed) *Handbook of the Philosophy of Science: Philosophy of Economics*. Amsterdam: Elsevier, 641–690. Available at SSRN.

Ariely, Dan. 2009. *Predictably Irrational: The Hidden Forces That Shape Our Decisions*. Revised Edition. New York: HarperCollins.

Ariely, Dan and Loewenstein, George. 2006. "The Heat of the Moment: The Effect of Sexual Arousal on Sexual Decision Making," *Journal of Behavioral Decision Making*, 19, 87–98.

Camerer, Colin F. and Loewenstein, George. 2004. "Behavioral Economics: Past, Present, Future," in Camerer, Colin F., Loewenstein, George and Rabin, Matthew (eds) *Advances in Behavioral Economics*. Princeton: Princeton University Press, 3–51.

Chaudhuri, Ananish. 2009. *Experiments in Economics: Playing Fair with Money*. New York: Routledge.

Cory Jr, Gerald A. 1999. *The Reciprocal Modular Brain in Economics and Politics: Shaping the Rational and Moral Basis of Organization, Exchange and Choice*. New York: Kluwer Academic.

Guth, W., Schmittberger, R. and Schwarze, B. 1982. "An Experimental Analysis of Ultimatum Bargaining," *Journal of Economic Behavior and Organization*, 3, 367–388.

Kahneman, Daniel, Knetsch, Jack L. and Thaler, Richard H. 1986. "Fairness and the Assumptions of Economics," *Journal of Business*, 59(4), part 2: S285–300.

Kahneman, Daniel. 2011. *Thinking Fast and Slow*. New York: Farrar, Strauss, and Giroux.

Loewenstein, George. 1996. "Out of Control: Visceral Influences on Behavior," *Organizational Behavior and Human Decision Processes*, 65(3), March, 272–292.

Loewenstein, George. 2000. "Emotions in Economic Theory and Economic Behavior," *American Economic Review*, 90(2), May, 426–432.

Loewenstein, George and Lerner, Jennifer S. 2003. "The Role of Affect in Decision Making," in Davidson, R.J., Goldsmith, H.H. and Scherer, K.R. (eds) *Handbook of Affective Science*. Oxford: Oxford University Press, 619–642.

Lynne, Gary D., Czap, Natalia, Czap, Hans and Burbach, Mark. 2015. "Empathy Conservation: Toward Avoiding the Tragedy of the Commons," *Review of Behavioral Economics*, forthcoming.

MacLean, Paul D. 1990. *The Triune Brain in Evolution: Role in Paleocerebral Functions*. New York: Plenum Press.

Mullainathan, Sendhil and Thaler, Richard. 2000. "Behavioral Economics," M.I.T. Department of Economics Working Paper Series, September. Available online from the Social Science Research Network.

Rabin, Matthew. 1998. 'Psychology and Economics,' *Journal of Economic Literature*, 36(1), March, 11–46.

Rabin, Matthew. 2002. "A Perspective on Psychology and Economics," *European Economic Review*, 46, 657–685.

Rick, Scott and Loewenstein, George. 2008. "The Role of Emotion in Economic Behavior," in Lewis, Michael, Haviland-Jones, Jeannette M. and Barrett, Lisa Feldman (eds) *Handbook of Emotions*, 3rd Edition. New York: Guilford Press, 138–156.

Sen, Amartya. 1977. "Rational Fools: A Critique of the Behavioral Foundations of Economic Theory," *Philosophy and Public Affairs*, 6, 317–344.

Slovic, Paul, Finucane, Melissa, Peters, Ellen and MacGregor, Donald G. 2002. "The Affect Heuristic," in Gilovich, Thomas, Griffin, Dale and Kahneman, Daniel (eds) *Heuristics and Biases: The Psychology of Intuitive Judgment*. Cambridge: Cambridge University Press, 397–420.

Thaler, Richard H. 1996. "Doing Economics without *Homo Economicus*," in Medema, Steven G. and Samuels, Warren J. (eds) *Foundations of Research in Economics: How Do Economists Do Economics?* Cheltenham, UK and Brookfield, VT: Edward Elgar Publishing,, 227–237.

Thaler, Richard H. 2015. *Misbehaving: The Making of Behavioral Economics*. New York: Norton.

Tomer, John F. 2012. "Brain Physiology, Egoistic and Empathic Motivation, and Brain Plasticity: Toward a More Human Economics," 1, 76–90.

Weber, Roberto and Dawes, Robyn. 2005. "Behavioral Economics," in Smelser, Neil J. and Swedberg, Richard (eds) *The Handbook of Economic Sociology*. 2nd Edition Princeton: Princeton University Press, 90–108.

6 Behavioral finance

Behavioral finance (BF) is essentially BE applied to the financial arena. To a considerable extent, BF draws on insights and analyses from psychology as psychological economics (PE) does (see Chapter 4), but it also draws on insights from a variety of other social sciences. Besides the social sciences, BF's origins are in financial theory, particularly the theory related to the pricing of speculative assets such as stocks and bonds. To understand how BF emerged from standard financial theory, it is necessary to begin by explaining the concept of efficient markets.

Efficient markets

In an efficient financial market, the prices of financial assets like stocks equal the intrinsic (or fundamental) values of these assets. According to the Efficient Market Hypothesis (EMH), the intrinsic value of securities will always faithfully reflect all that can be known about their present conditions and future prospects (Malkiel 1999, p. 29). If follows that the intrinsic value of a stock will equal the present or discounted value of all the future dividends that an owner of the stock can expect to receive. These dividend expectations are those of rational, independent investors whose expectations are based on all relevant publicly available information (Shleifer 2000, pp. 1–2). Similar to neoclassical economics (NE), the EMH assumes that the people who invest are not only extremely rational but also "cunningly efficient processors of financial information" (Shiller 2005, pp. xx–xxi). According to proponents of EMH, U.S. bond and stock markets are actually efficient (Shleifer 2000, p. 1). In these efficient markets, it is not possible to forecast changes in stock prices. This is because these stock prices change only in response to news (by definition, not previously known information). When news occurs, this causes rational investors to revise their expectations and, consequently, the estimates of their securities' intrinsic value. In such markets, security values and prices follow random paths because relevant news occurs randomly (Shleifer 2000, p. 3). When good news occurs, investors respond by attempting to buy more of the security, and prices are bid up; and when bad news occurs, they attempt to sell, and prices are bid down. When there are many attentive investors, security prices always quickly, perhaps instantaneously, adjust to their intrinsic values. As an example, if a company is worth $100 million, its stock will trade for $100 million, and if there are 10 million shares outstanding, the price per share will be $10. In the absence of news about the company, the price will not change. When news occurs, there will be momentary price changes as investors place buy and sell orders consistent with their new expectations.[1]

Is it possible to make a profit trading stock in an efficient market, i.e., beat the market? No! An investor in an efficient market "cannot hope to consistently beat the market, and the vast resources that such investors dedicate to analysing, picking, and trading securities are wasted. Better to passively hold the market portfolio, and to forget active money management altogether" (Shleifer 2000, p. 1). This is because security prices in these markets vary randomly, and there is no way to reliably predict them (Thaler 2015, p. 207). One kind of evidence consistent with this is that "professional money managers perform no better than simple market averages" (p. 207).

It is noteworthy that proponents of the EMH developed a number of theoretical arguments explaining why the EMH would hold even if investors were not independent and rational (Shleifer 2000, p. 2). First, if a substantial number of investors were irrational but their trading activities were uncorrelated with each other, then, it is argued, their trades will cancel each other out, and the markets will still be efficient. A second argument is based on arbitrage. Arbitrage might, for example, work in the case where the actions of irrational investors have caused a security to become overvalued, i.e., caused its price to exceed its intrinsic value. This presumably would create an opportunity for rational arbitrageurs, the "smart money," to sell the overvalued security short. This would involve borrowing the overvalued asset, selling it, and returning it after the price had fallen. Such an action would lower the security's price, presumably bringing its price back to its intrinsic value. Arbitrage can also work to eliminate overvaluation using other more complicated maneuvers. And, of course, arbitrage, in a similar and opposite way, can work to eliminate undervaluation.

The EMH was conceived in the 1960s, and Eugene Fama's statement of this hypothesis in 1970 was extremely influential. In the 1970s, "the EMH turned into an enormous theoretical and empirical success. Academics developed powerful theoretical reasons why the hypothesis should hold. More impressively, a vast array of empirical findings quickly emerged – nearly all of them supporting the hypothesis" (Shleifer 2000, p. 1). And "in 1978, Michael Jensen [referring to the EMH] declared that there is no other proposition in economics which has more solid empirical evidence supporting it" (p. 1).

Problems with the efficient market hypothesis

By the early 1980s, a few finance researchers had begun to recognize the problematic nature of the EMH. Arguably, the most important of these researchers was Robert Shiller who later became recognized as the leading practitioner of behavioral finance. Shiller's early "concern was whether . . . [stock prices] show excess volatility relative to what would be predicted by the efficient markets model" (Shiller 2003, p. 84). The important question was whether the departures from market efficiency were small or whether they were large enough to "call into question the basic underpinnings of the entire EMH" (p. 84). What Shiller found strongly "implied that [a great proportion of the] changes in prices occur for no fundamental reason at all" (p. 84). For example, one kind of interesting, recurring pattern of stock price behavior that violates market efficiency is the speculative bubble. According to Shiller (2013, pp. 460–461), a bubble is defined as:

> a situation in which news of price increases spurs investor enthusiasm which spreads by psychological contagion from person to person, in the process amplifying stories that might justify the price increase in a larger and larger class of investors, who, despite doubts about the real value of the investment, are drawn to it partly through envy of others' successes and partly through a gambler's excitement.

In other words, the term bubble is associated with situations in which prices have risen way beyond what reasonable people would expect. Further, the word bubble suggests that prices in this market may be reaching to or near to their peak, and if so, the bubble is extremely likely to burst or crash, at which point the prices will fall rapidly. Note that efficient market enthusiasts doubt that bubbles exist and can typically offer alternative explanations for the large price rises (p. 461).

An opposite phenomenon that is inconsistent with market efficiency is what happened on October 19, 1987. On that day, the stock market crashed, "the Dow Jones Industrial Average fell by 22.6 percent – the largest one day percentage drop in history – without any apparent news. Although the event caused an aggressive search for the news that may have caused it, no persuasive culprit could be identified" (Shleifer 2000, p. 20). This is a real puzzle because the EMH not only implies that stock prices change in response to news but it also implies that stock prices will not react significantly in the absence of news.

In the early 1980s, Robert Shiller (1981) sought to examine aggregate stock market patterns in order to determine whether they were consistent with the EMH. His research used data from many years to make visual portrayals of the volatility of stock market prices compared to that of stocks' intrinsic values. The resulting graph provided very convincing evidence of the lack of efficiency in aggregate stock market prices (Shiller 2013, pp. 467–471). The graph compared two sets of data. One was Standard & Poor's real stock prices (deflated by the U.S. consumer price index) from 1871 to the present. The second set of data consisted of Shiller's estimates of the present value of future real dividends per share discounted at a constant rate (p. 467). (This data series was used as an estimate of these stocks' intrinsic values.) To construct the dividend series, Shiller had to estimate the value of real dividends for future periods. To make these estimates, he assumed that future dividends would grow at the same rate as past dividends. Because Shiller's figures on future dividends were only rough estimates, he calculated the dividend series using several different assumptions. Regardless of the assumptions, the plot of the present value of dividends over time appears smooth, pretty much like a steady exponential growth line. On the other hand, his plot of stock market prices over time is very volatile, showing dramatic, sudden shifts above and below the dividend line. The reaction of people who have observed this figure with these two series is that it is entirely inconsistent with the efficient market model. If the stock market were efficient, and if the smooth present value of dividends data were a reasonable estimate of stocks' intrinsic values, the stock price series should largely coincide with the dividend plot (p. 469). But this is not the case at all. Why are the stock price data so volatile? When Shiller did this research in the early 1980s, he was not in a position to give a good answer to this question. However, it did seem very unlikely to him that all these large aggregate stock price changes were related to the occurrence of important news stories.

The aggregate stock market performance from 1994 to 2000 was of particular interest to Shiller and many others. His book *Irrational Exuberance* (Shiller 2005) pays considerable attention to this period. The book was named after a phrase used by Alan Greenspan, Chairman of the Federal Reserve Board, in his televised speech in Washington, DC on December 5, 1996 (p. 1). Greenspan used the term to characterize investors at that time who seemed to him to be overly enthusiastic about buying stocks, which contributed to bidding up their prices. Although Greenspan's speech was followed immediately by large price declines in stock markets around the world, the trend to higher stock prices soon resumed. "The Dow Jones Industrial Average ... stood at around 3600 in early 1994 ... [and] the Dow peaked at 11723 in January 14, 2000" (p. 2). Shiller considers this period to be the biggest historical example of a speculative bubble. "The stock market increases for 1994 to 2000 could not obviously be justified in any reasonable terms" (p. 2). Although stock market prices more than tripled, basic economic indicators such as gross domestic product rose less than 40 percent, and corporate profits rose less than 60 percent. In 2000, the bubble burst. The whole stock market episode from 1994–2000 constitutes strong evidence of a bubble, and it is evidence against the EMH; but many would not consider this to be a test of the EMH. Strictly speaking, it is almost impossible to test whether a market is efficient because intrinsic values are not observable (Thaler 2015, p. 206). It is interesting to note that Shiller warned of the excessive rise in stock prices in 1996, but the stock market bubble continued expanding for four more years. As Thaler (2015, pp. 234–235) points out, Shiller was wrong for four years before he was right. This means "it is much easier to detect that we may be in a bubble than it is to say when it will pop, and investors who attempt to make money by timing market turns are rarely successful" (p. 236).

Besides stock market bubbles and excess volatility, there are a number of other interesting anomalies that do not square with efficient market theory. One such anomaly is that during 1937 to 1969, cheap stocks, ones with the lowest P/Es, price divided by earnings per share, substantially outperformed the expensive stocks with the highest P/Es (Thaler 2015, p. 220). "From 1937 to 1969, a $10,000 investment in the cheap stocks would have increased in value to $66,900, while the expensive stock portfolio would only have increased to $25,300" (p. 220). A second anomaly is that the stocks of small firms outperform the stocks of large firms (Shleifer 2000, pp. 18–19). "Between 1926 and 1996, for example, the compounded annual return on the largest decile of New

York Stock Exchange stocks has been 9.84 percent, compared to 13.83 percent on the smallest decile of stocks" (p. 18). A third interesting anomaly is that portfolios of the best performing stocks, "winners," over, say, five years underperform portfolios of the worst performers, "losers," in the following five years. "Over the five-year period after we formed our portfolios, the losers outperformed the market by about 30 percent while the winners did worse than the market by about 10 percent" (Thaler 2015, p. 223). If markets were truly efficient, none of these anomalies should have existed, even for short periods of time. Note that these anomalies are akin to the popular approach to investing called value investing in which portfolios of stocks with the lowest ratio of market value of a company's equity to the accounting book value of its assets are selected (Shleifer 2000, p. 19). Such stocks are presumably relatively cheap and underappreciated. Again, if markets are really efficient, the value approach should not work.

Behavioral finance

Robert Shiller's (1981) paper dealt with the problems of market efficiency theory utilizing econometric analyses of time series data on prices, dividends, and earnings. After much research had been done in this vein by Shiller and others, the focus of academic discussion in the 1990s shifted toward developing models that utilized psychology and other social sciences to explain why financial markets are often not efficient. In other words, the field of behavioral finance began to develop (Shiller 2003, p. 90). Researchers were tiring of simply documenting anomalies and departures from efficiency. The next important step was to explain this anomalous financial behavior. Shiller, at the urging of Richard Thaler, became convinced of the need to adopt a behavioral perspective and to "embrace the heretical idea that social phenomena might influence stock prices" in ways beyond the purview of standard economics (Thaler 2015, p. 233).

Before explaining about the behavioral aspect of people's financial market activities, it is important to explain why arbitrage often does not work to eliminate the over or under valuation of securities. Recall that according to the EMH, the role of arbitrage is to bring prices back to their intrinsic values via the rational buying and selling activities of "smart money" investors. If arbitrage is to work, for example, to lower security prices, the "arbitrageurs must be able to buy 'the same or essentially similar' securities that are not overpriced" (Shleifer

2000, p. 13). This is frequently not possible. Moreover, arbitrage typically involves complicated procedures. For such reasons, arbitrage is generally a risky endeavor, and thus, relatively few investors are willing to engage in it (pp. 14–16). The upshot is that "limited arbitrage . . . explains why markets may remain inefficient" when investors who are in some sense irrational cause security prices to depart from their intrinsic values (pp. 24–25).

If arbitrage cannot be relied upon to eliminate the deviation of security prices from their intrinsic values, these deviations can be both very substantial and very lasting. To understand why these lapses from market efficiency occur in the first place, it is necessary to turn to behavioral finance theories (many borrowed from BE). There are many of these theories, however, "there is no single unifying model of BF" (Shleifer 2000, p. 25).

The first BF theory considered here relates to how stock market "noise" can lead to irrational investor behavior. At any given time, there is a lot going on in the stock market; prices are always changing to some degree. Some of these price changes are related to genuine news, the kind of new information that would cause a rational individual (an econ) to change his/her expectations regarding a stock. Other price changes are merely due to noise, an "occurrence that does not qualify as news" (Thaler 2015, p. 240). Some stock investors, especially unsophisticated individual investors, often make trades on the basis of noise.[2] Depending on the outcomes of such trades, these investors may experience shifting moods of optimism or pessimism (p. 241). These mood changes have been referred to as "investor sentiment;" they are associated with investors becoming either depressed and scared or becoming more confident. These sentiments can affect the path of stock market prices even though they are not related to changes in stocks' intrinsic values. When investors react to noise, they are, strictly speaking, not being rational; they are in effect overreacting to what is happening in the financial market.

"One of the oldest theories about financial markets, expressed long ago in newspapers and magazines rather than scholarly journals" is feedback theory that explain bubbles (Shiller 2003, p. 91). The essence of feedback theory is that some initial security price increases, possibly due to noise, cause yet higher prices as other investors respond and demand the security. "This second round of price increases feeds back again into a third round and then a fourth, and so on" (Shiller 2005,

p. 68). In essence, the initial price increases create successes for some investors, attracting public attention, enthusiasm, heightened expectations for more price increases, and perhaps envy on the part of investors who have been left out (Shiller 2003, p. 91). One version of feedback theory involves adaptive expectations in which "past price increases generate expectations of further price increases" (Shiller 2005, p. 69). In another slightly different version, the past price increases cause increased investor confidence. In some cases, the feedback is price-to-price feedback. In other cases, it could be price-to-GDP-to-price feedback or even price-to-corporate-earnings-to-price feedback (p. 79). At some point, of course, speculative bubbles fueled by feedbacks will come to a stop, and the bubble will burst when "investors no longer think prices will continue to rise and therefore no longer see a good reason to hold the stock" (Shiller 2005, p. 71). Feedback theory can also apply in the downward direction (a negative bubble) as initial price declines create more and more discouragement among investors (p. 71).

It is hard to get good solid evidence supporting feedback theory. One pertinent kind of evidence comes from the example of Ponzi schemes (Shiller 2005, pp. 74–76). "In a Ponzi scheme, the manager of the scheme promises to make large profits for investors by investing their money. But little or no investment of contributors' funds in any real assets is made. Instead, the manager pays off the initial investors with the proceeds of a sale to a second round of investors," and so on (p. 74).

Typically the Ponzi scheme manager tells investors a plausible story about the scheme's investments and how great profit can be made. Such schemes are, in a way, controlled experiments that demonstrate how feedback works. Feedback is involved because the "Ponzi scheme entices initial investors . . . to tell their success stories to another round of investors, who then invest even more in the scheme, allowing the hoaxer to pay off the second round investors," and so on (p. 74). The success of Ponzi schemes derives from the feedback, i.e., "the powerful effect on people's thinking of seeing others having made substantial sums of money" (p. 76). In the Ponzi scheme, the role of feedback is very clear, unlike in ordinary investing situations.

When large, long-lasting stock market bubbles occur, it is notable that they typically give rise to "new era" stories that justify the high prices (Shiller 2005, pp. 106–131). When the stock market is riding high, it is easy for many people to accept the proposition that the future will be brighter or less uncertain than the past (p. 106). In the mid to late 1990s, the arrival of the Internet and the boom in high-tech industries led many to believe that fundamental economic change was occurring and that productivity would grow at a faster rate, justifying the rapid growth in stock prices (pp. 106–108). This new era story is only the latest of many. New era thinking "is part of the process by which a boom may be sustained and amplified – part of the feedback mechanism" creating and sustaining the bubble (p. 108). Whenever the market reaches a new high, public speakers, writers, and other prominent people suddenly appear, armed with explanations for the apparent optimism seen in the market" (p. 108). Only later after the bubble has burst is it possible to see with clarity the flaws in the most recent new era stories.

Insights deriving from psychological economics (see Chapter 4) are important to BF. Accordingly, when people who are investors make judgments, they frequently are biased, and their financial decisions all too frequently are irrational. Investors like other people use their intuition and typically utilize the representative heuristic. This means that "people tend to make judgments in uncertain situations by looking for familiar patterns and assuming that future patterns will resemble past ones, often without sufficient consideration of the reasons for the pattern or the probability of the pattern repeating itself" (Shiller 2005, pp. 153–154). One such common error is that people tend to match the current stock price pattern with well-known common pattern categories without paying sufficient attention to the probabilities involved (Shiller 2003, pp. 93–94). People also tend to see stock price patterns in truly random sequences (Shleifer 2000, p. 129). In addition, people basing their judgments on observations utilizing small sample sizes tend to identify and infer a definite stock price pattern too quickly (Barberis and Thaler 2003, p. 1067).

Another way people's judgments and decision making can get them into financial trouble is due to their overconfidence. People's "basic tendency toward overconfidence appears to be a robust human character trait" that manifests frequently in financial markets (Shiller 2005, p. 153). First, overconfidence contributes to investors' tendency to trade too frequently in speculative markets (Shiller 2013, p. 485). Second, due to their overconfidence, investors may have strong beliefs about financial events they think are certain to occur but research shows actually occur only 80 percent of the time (Barberis and Thaler 2003, p. 1065). Such investors may also have strong beliefs about events they think cannot possibly occur but research shows actually occur

20 percent of the time (p. 1065). Relatedly, it is not uncommon for overconfident investors "to believe they know when a market move will take place, even if they generally believe as an intellectual matter that stock prices are not forecastable" (Shiller 2005, p. 154), and even if they believe that investing on the basis of market timing is extremely difficult. Finally, it seems clear that "overconfidence in one's own intuitive judgments plays a fundamental role" in understanding speculative bubbles, positive or negative (p. 155).

Another psychological economics topic applicable to BF is anchoring. Does the stock market have an anchor? Financial assets in speculative markets like the stock market very often do not trade at their intrinsic or fundamental values. And since people trading in these markets generally do not know if the market is under or over valued, these markets' prices are not clearly "anchored" to a certain level (Shiller 2005, pp. 147–148). There are, however, psychological anchors that tend to provide some degree of constraint or stability to the market. Shiller considers two types of anchors: quantitative and moral (p. 148). Chapter 4 provided a general discussion of quantitative anchors. In market situations that are ambiguous, investors can be influenced by whatever available quantities are at hand. For example, typical quantitative anchors might be convenient financial numbers such as 1) the most recently remembered past price of a stock, 2) the level of a prominent index of stock prices such as the Dow Jones Industrial Average, 3) the magnitude of price changes in other stocks, or 4) price to earnings (P/E) ratios in relation to other firms' P/E ratios (pp. 148–149). People use these anchors in making judgments about particular stock prices and about the level of stock prices, and these judgments influence their decision making. Because of this quantitative anchoring, stock prices tend to be less variable than otherwise. Moral anchors relate to the intuitive force of stories and reasons concerning 1) why people invest in the stock market vis-a-vis alternative uses of their funds and 2) why they are investing in the stocks of the particular companies they have chosen (pp. 148–152). People want stories and reasons to justify their stock decisions. People also want to feel morally superior because they are committed to investing and accumulating wealth over a lifetime. The ethical ideals and convictions of investors related to the above considerations in some ways constrain and influence, i.e., anchor, the level of the market. There are a fair number of other psychological and economic theories that have been applied in BF. For instance, investors' judgment and decision making are influenced by how they frame the market situations they confront and by the types of mental accounting they employ. At times, investors are overly optimistic and engage in wishful thinking, even magical thinking. At other times, they may have a tendency to be overly conservative, tending to cling to their prior estimates of a market situation. Further, investors may be loss averse, avoiding stock market gambles in which losses loom large. All these behaviors and many more can at times play a role in causing speculative markets to depart from efficiency.

Conclusion

The behavioral finance research in which Robert Shiller has led the way has done much to demonstrate the weaknesses of efficient market theory. "Efficient market theory may lead to drastically incorrect interpretations of events such as major stock market bubbles" (Shiller 2003, p. 101). On the other hand, efficient market theory has some value in its implications about how to invest in the stock market. And as Shiller has pointed out, the "theoretical models of efficient markets have their place as illustrations or characterizations of an ideal world, [even though] we cannot maintain them in their pure form as accurate descriptors of actual markets" (p. 102). To describe the actual workings of speculative markets, the insights and evidence from BF are essential because they "help us understand, for example, that the worldwide stock market boom, and then crash after 2000, had its origins in human foibles and arbitrary feedback relations and must have generated a real and substantial misallocation of resources," not to mention considerable human suffering in its aftermath (p. 102). Clearly, BF, which integrates economics and financial theory with the findings of psychology and other social sciences, has contributed greatly to understanding how financial markets really work, an understanding that could not have been gained without the contributions of interdisciplinary researchers, especially behavioral economists.

NOTES

1 Finance researchers distinguish three forms of the EMH. The first is weak form efficiency in which the relevant information used by investors is the past prices and returns of the security. The second form, known as the semi-strong form, is where the investors are using any publicly available information. In the third form of efficiency known as strong form, investors trade using all the above information plus information that is not yet known by most market participants but which sometimes leaks out. The latter information is generally called insider information (Shleifer 2000, p. 6).

2 Noise traders are making their trades on the basis of supposedly irrelevant factors and are idiots! (Thaler 2015, p. 240).

References

Barberis, Nicholas and Thaler, Richard. 2003. "A Survey of Behavioral Finance," in Constantinides, George M., Harris, Milton, Stulz, Rene (eds) *Handbook of the Economics of Finance, Volume 1B, Financial Markets and Asset Pricing*. Amsterdam: Elsevier 1054–1092.

Malkiel, Burton G. 1999. *A Random Walk Down Wall Street*. New York: Norton.

Shiller, Robert J. 1981. "Do Stock Prices Move Too Much to be Justified by Subsequent Changes in Dividends," *American Economic Review*, 71(3), 421–436.

Shiller, Robert J. 2003. "From Efficient Market Theory to Behavioral Finance," *Journal of Economic Perspectives*, 17(1), 83–104.

Shiller, Robert J. 2005. *Irrational Exuberance*. New York: Doubleday.

Shiller, Robert J. 2013. "Speculative Asset Prices," Nobel Prize in Economic Science Lecture, December 8, 459–501.

Shleifer, Andrei. 2000. *Inefficient Markets: An Introduction to Behavioral Finance*. Oxford: Oxford University Press.

Thaler, Richard H. 2015. *Misbehaving: The Making of Behavioral Economics*. New York: Norton.

7 Behavioral economics, public policy, and nudging

Public policy, behavioral economics, and human nature

The issue addressed in this chapter is what can behavioral economics (BE) contribute to the improvement of public policy. To understand this, one must start with how BE differs from neoclassical economics (NE). The essence, of course, as earlier chapters have explained, is that BE's understanding of human behavior is very different from that of NE. In short, humans are quite different from econs. Unlike econs, who are assumed to be unfailingly rational and unemotional, humans have a variety of cognitive biases such as loss aversion, status quo bias, anchoring, framing, confirmation bias, overconfidence, saliency bias, inconsistent preferences over time, and others. Moreover, humans are not only boundedly rational; they are also bounded in their willpower and self-interest. Relatedly, humans typically use a variety of rules of thumb in decision making, especially when decision situations are not simple (Tomer 2013, p. 93; Low 2012). In other words, humans by their very nature have limited cognitive abilities along with many identifiable biases that impair their judgments and decision making. Understanding those human limitations is a key to developing policies that are in many ways a substantial improvement over the policies that derive directly from NE thinking.

The problem with neoclassical economic decision making and the promise of behavioral economics

According to standard versions of NE, individuals are assumed to make rational decisions by impassively weighing the costs and benefits of alternative courses of action and by choosing the alternative that maximizes their satisfaction. Thus, economists typically believe that practically any problem can be fixed, simply by adopting government measures that appropriately change the incentives (the expected costs and benefits) faced by individuals and businesses (Low 2012, p. 2). It is all a matter of "getting the incentives right." With the right incentives, the problem will be resolved because people will then make the desired (and predicted) decisions. In the case of problems involving negative externalities, the solution involves causing decision makers to experience, and thereby take into account, the costs that they are imposing on the rest of society. This could involve the imposition of taxes on vehicle use, on environmental emissions, gambling, cigarette smoking, or alcohol consumption. Such measures can help, but in many cases, do not work so well. The difficulty is that people's decision making processes are more complicated than doing cost-benefit calculations. Typically, decision makers are influenced by a variety of psychological, sociological, and environmental factors. As a consequence, people's actions cannot be explained simply by standard economic considerations. If people were entirely rational and only considered costs and benefits, standard economic explanations would suffice. In that case, people would always save enough for retirement, buy sufficient health insurance coverage, and buy the energy-efficient appliances that save them money (pp. 3–4). All too often, humans do not do those things. They frequently decide not to do things that have long-term large benefits and relatively small short-term costs. Humans also frequently fail to eat healthily and exercise sufficiently, favor instant gratification, and depart from perfect economic rationality in other ways. Therefore, policymakers need an alternative to standard economics; they need BE because it provides a relatively rigorous way to incorporate accurate understanding concerning human motivation and decision making processes. Using BE, policymakers can develop more effective policies that can allow them to attain greater success.

The philosophy of libertarian paternalism

To appreciate how BE can contribute to improving public policy, it is necessary to understand the philosophy of libertarian paternalism. The paternalistic aspect of the philosophy connotes governing in a manner similar to how a father relates to his children; the father is concerned for his children and makes efforts to improve their well-being. Paternalism in government policy connotes an attitude of concern for the well-being of those who are governed. Some people view paternalism negatively because they associate it with hard-nosed coercion. But as Thaler and Sunstein (2003, pp. 175–177; 2009, pp. 4–6) explain, the paternalistic aspect of a government's or private entity's policy is inevitable and need not be coercive or intrusive. The other half of the libertarian paternalism philosophy, libertarianism, connotes the view that people should be fully free in all their thoughts and actions. The combination of libertarianism and paternalism produces a "libertarian paternalism [that] is a relatively weak, soft, and nonintrusive type of paternalism because choices are not blocked, fenced off, or significantly burdened" (p. 5). Libertarian paternalistic policies are "ones that maintain or increase freedom of choice" (p. 5). Such policies "make it easy for people to go their own way" even when the paternalistic aspect of policy is trying "to influence people's behavior in order to make their lives longer, healthier, and better" (p. 5). Libertarian paternalistic policies are needed because of humans' limited mental capacities. Humans all too frequently are predictably irrational, i.e., they "make inferior choices, choices they would change if they had complete information, unlimited cognitive abilities, and no lack of willpower" (Thaler and Sunstein 2003, p. 175).

Nudge: the essence and an example

In light of human foibles, what should a libertarian paternalist do? Why not use a nudge in order to improve people's well-being? A nudge is an action that "alters people's behavior in a predictable way without forbidding any options or significantly changing their economic incentives. To count as a mere nudge, the intervention must be easy and cheap to avoid" (Thaler and Sunstein 2009, p. 6). One easy-to-understand example of a nudge takes place in a school cafeteria where students choose their displayed lunch foods as they pass down the cafeteria line.[1] The cafeteria management heretofore has not given any thought to the display and arrangement of the foods. Recently, at this school, parents and some school leaders have expressed concern about whether the students who eat at the cafeteria are eating sufficiently nutritious meals. Reflecting this concern, the cafeteria manager has decided to do a study to determine whether the display and arrangement of the food is having an adverse effect on the nutritious level of students' food choices. The study's findings are of interest. First, they find that too often desserts have been located first and displayed prominently in the cafeteria line. Second, they find that healthy vegetables have typically not been well displayed nor given prominent locations. And, third, less nutritious "fast foods" have often been placed at eye level locations and displayed in a salient way. By experimenting, they further find that by making better decisions regarding the location and display of food from the standpoint of nutrition, they can increase students' consumption of healthy foods and decrease their consumption of unhealthy foods. Based on these findings, the cafeteria manager decided to change the display and location of the food in order to improve the nutritious level of students' lunch choices. As a result of these changes, the students' choices are found to be 25 percent more nutritious than they had been. Clearly, the students at this school have been nudged. Arguably, this is a successful nudge, and the students are better off as a result.

Choice architecture

In the above example, the cafeteria manager has become a choice architect. "A choice architect has the responsibility for organizing the context in which people make decisions" (Thaler and Sunstein 2009, p. 3). There are many features in any environment, whether noticed or not, that influence people's decisions. Choice architects who make decisions about environmental features often have a crucial effect on people's choice making (Thaler, Sunstein, and Balz 2010, p. 428). People in many different fields and situations can be choice architects. For example, people who design the ballot that voters use to choose candidates, people who design the form that new employers fill out to enroll in the company's health care plan, the person who designs the menu in a restaurant, "doctors describing the available treatments to patients, . . . parents explaining the educational options available to a teenager," even traditional building architects, are choice architects (p. 1). It is important to note that all the features of an environment's design influence people's decisions in some way. Thus, the choice architect has the responsibility of picking out and using features that will influence decision making in a particular desirable way but not in some other way. Ideally, choice architects choose features that nudge people's choices in a way that makes their lives longer, healthier, and better (Thaler and Sunstein 2009, p. 5).

The need for nudges

Why are nudges needed? They are generally needed because people are busy and trying to get along in a complex world. Thus people do not have enough time or attention to think deeply about all the different choices they have to make (Thaler and Sunstein 2009, p. 37). Consequently, many people will appreciate helpful nudges. People need nudges more in certain kinds of situations. In general, "people will need nudges for decisions that are difficult and rare, for which they do not get prompt feedback, and when they have trouble translating aspects of the situation into terms that they can easily understand" (p. 74). This means that nudges are likely to be more important with respect to choosing a college, choosing a career, and buying a house, but not so important with regard to weekly grocery shopping. With regard to taste, food shopping generally gives relatively clear, quick feedback, but with respect to certain aspects of long-term health, the food feedback may be very slow and unclear (pp. 75–77). Overall, the "goal of many nudges is to make life simpler, safer, or easier for people to navigate" (Sunstein 2014, p. 2). "Many nudges are intended to ensure that people do not struggle when they seek to interact with government or achieve their goals" (p. 2).

Nudging increased saving

There is plenty of evidence that many people are not saving enough for their retirement. This is true despite the fact that governments have passed laws creating tax-favored savings accounts such as IRAs and 401(k)s to encourage personal savings (Thaler and Sunstein 2009, p. 105). Why do many people save too little? There are two main reasons why dealing with retirement saving is not easy. First, it is no easy task for people "to figure out how much they will need when they retire and then save up just enough to enjoy a comfortable retirement [for the rest of their lives] without sacrificing too much while they are still working" (p. 106). Second, it is also not easy for people to muster up enough will power to carry out their savings plan. And, of course, they need to do these two things at the same time that they are dealing with many other competing demands for their money, time, and attention. To help people increase their retirement savings, two important nudges have been suggested: 1) automatic enrollment in savings plans and 2) the Save More Tomorrow program.

Adopting automatic enrollment in a saving plan simply involves changing the saving plan's default option from automatic non-enrollment, which has typically been the default in many organizations. A default option is the option that will result if the chooser does nothing. Because of inertia and people's natural tendency to stay with the status quo, many people just go along with the default option chosen by their organization. With automatic enrollment, people will be enrolled in this saving plan unless they opt-out. With automatic non-enrollment, people have to opt-in (make an explicit choice) to be enrolled in the plan (Thaler and Sunstein 2009, pp. 110–111). There is considerable evidence that automatic enrollment works to raise the number of people participating in the savings plans offered by organizations. Moreover, "the fact that so few people drop out [if they were to exercise the opt-out at a later date] does suggest that workers are not suddenly discovering, to their dismay, that they are saving more than they had wanted" (p. 111). The evidence cited by Thaler and Sunstein (pp. 110–111) is convincing that this type of nudge gets people to save more and thereby improves their well-being.

Save More Tomorrow (SMT) is the name of an innovative nudging plan developed by Thaler and Benartzi (2004). This plan raises people's saving rates much more than has typically occurred using only automatic enrollment. SMT involves an automatic escalation of people's savings contributions. To understand why the choice architecture of SMT works, it is necessary to consider a number of aspects of human nature that tend to defeat people's efforts to save more: 1) although people may believe they should save more and they plan to do so, they rarely follow through; 2) it is easier for people to agree to changes some time in the future rather than in the present; 3) people are loss averse especially with respect to take home pay (it hurts them a lot to see their paychecks go down); and 4) people are averse to change (Thaler and Sunstein 2009, p. 114). To participate in SMT, people must "commit themselves, in advance, to a series of [saving] contribution increases timed to coincide with pay raises" (p. 115). Up to a certain rate of saving, their savings rate will increase each time their pay increases. This means that even as their rate of savings increases, their take home pay continues to increase (they will not experience a loss of pay). Because people joining the SMT program are making a commitment that starts in the future, and because they never experience losses, they are more willing to commit to it. Furthermore, this commitment is reinforced when people see the higher saving result. The particular choice architecture of the SMT program is what leads to dramatically favorable savings outcomes. Because of this, "many retirement plan administrators have adopted the SMT idea" including leading companies such as Vanguard, T. Rowe Price, TIAA-CREF, and Fidelity (p. 116). When automatic enrollment and SMT are used together, the combined nudges toward greater saving have been very effective and seem to have improved people's well-being.

Ten important types of nudges

Behavioral economists have in recent years developed a wide range
of nudges, and the number and variety of them are growing. To get a
better handle on the types of nudges, Cass Sunstein (2014, pp. 585–587)
has put together a helpful list of ten important categories of nudges:

(1)   default rules (e.g. automatic enrollment in programs including
      education, health, and savings)
(2)   simplification (complexity is a serious problem . . . it causes
      confusion . . . can increase expense. The benefits of important
      government programs are greatly reduced because of undue
      complexity)
(3)   uses of social norms (emphasize what most people do, e.g.,
      'most people vote . . . pay taxes on time')
(4)   increases in ease and convenience (e.g., make low-cost options
      or healthy foods visible . . . make choices easy . . . reduce
      barriers)
(5)   disclosure (e.g., disclose environmental costs of products . . .
      disclose the full cost of certain credit cards . . .)
(6)   warnings, graphic or otherwise (e.g., warnings of risk that
      trigger people's attention . . . cigarettes)
(7)   precommitment strategies (get people to commit to a certain
      course of action such as smoking cessation)
(8)   reminders (e.g., use email or text messages for bills, obligations
      and appointments)
(9)   eliciting implementation intentions (increases people's likeli-
      hood of engaging in an activity)
(10) informing people of the nature and consequences of their own
      past choices (e.g., if people had better information on their past
      health care choices and expenditures, their behavior can shift).

Nudges in relation to other government efforts

Governments do many things and do them in many different ways.
The instruments of government policy include mandates, bans, economic incentives and disincentives (including subsidies, fees, and
taxes), non-fiscal incentives and disincentives, restricting choice, and
nudges (Sunstein 2014, p. 1; UK House of Lords 2011). Some government efforts are focused on changing people's problematic behavior.
These efforts include measures that inform, persuade, and promote

(p. 2). With regard to behavioral change, nudges, as generally conceived, do not attempt to influence behavior by getting people to engage in effortful deliberation regarding their behavior (p. 12). As explained earlier in this chapter, nudges are mainly understood to work as people respond in desirable ways to the environmental features introduced by choice architects. So how do BE-related policy measures such as nudges fit together with standard policy measures? Consider Singapore, a nation that has developed a uniquely successful approach to government policy. In Singapore, policymakers attempt to use government programs that utilize a mix of instruments, both those based on efficiency considerations, ones deriving from standard economics, and those based on psychological considerations, ones deriving from BE (Low 2012, pp. 6–8). How do the two types of government measures fit together when governments are trying to tackle a large socio-economic problem? In Tomer's (2013) research that focused on the kind of efforts that would be necessary to resolve the problem of obesity, the government policy recommendations included the use of both conventional economic incentives (e.g., taxing unhealthy foods) and social and psychological measures designed to influence people's behavior and values. Also of interest is the UK House of Lords Report on "Behaviour Change" (2011, pp. 9–12) in which interventions that use standard rules and regulations were contrasted with "non-regulatory" interventions that use the "sciences of human behavior" in their design. The latter includes nudging. The UK report's authors, while interested in and acknowledging the benefits of the nudging approach, favor a governmental approach that uses a combination of standard regulatory approaches and newer behaviorally influenced approaches.

Are nudges ethical and acceptable?

The nudge concept has been criticized on ethical grounds. The main criticism is that government nudges could be excessively intrusive in the life of the nudged individual. Conceivably, nudges could involve outright manipulation and trickery, thereby coercing Nudgees to do things that are not in their best interests. Nudging of this nature presumably would be covert and would not respect the autonomy of Nudgees, not allowing them to be free to do what they want and to learn from their experiences. To prevent such adverse nudging, proponents of nudging advocate that nudging (especially government nudging) should be transparent and open (Sunstein 2014, p. 2). "The public

should be able to review and scrutinize nudges no less than government actions of any kind" (p. 2). To provide the necessary transparency,
this "might mean telling people about a [nudge] intervention directly
or it might mean ensuring that a perceptive person could discern for
themselves that a [nudge] intervention had been implemented" (UK
House of Lords 2011, p. 13). The ethical acceptability of a particular
nudge will, of course, depend to a considerable extent on the degree to
which it intrudes on a Nudgee's life and the degree to which the nudge
is covert. But, equally as important, the ethical acceptability of any
nudge will depend on the public's perception of the importance of the
nudge and whether the public had in a sense given its permission for
the nudge intervention (p. 14). In the final analysis, the nudge's ethical
and public acceptability will depend to a considerable degree on the
size "of the problem the [nudge] intervention is designed to solve and
the evidence that it will be effective in doing so" (p. 15).

Good nudges require evidence

It has become widely recognized that developing valuable nudges and
other behaviorally informed policy instruments requires evidence
and often requires experimentation. The need for evidence-based
policies, especially related to energy-efficient products and smoking
cessation, is recognized by the UK House of Lords (2011, p. 6). They
recognize that their evaluation of government nudge interventions
should make good use of behavioral disciplines including neuroscience, psychology, sociology, and behavioral economics in order that
they reflect a realistic understanding of how people will respond to
nudges (p. 8). According to Sunstein (2014, p. 585):

> it is exceedingly important to rely on evidence rather than intuitions, anec-
> dotes, wishful thinking, or dogmas .... Some policies, including some
> nudges, seem promising in the abstract, but turn out to fail in practice.
> Empirical tests, including randomized controlled trials, are indispensable.
> Bad surprises certainly are possible, including unintended adverse conse-
> quences, and sensible policymakers must try to anticipate such surprises
> in advance (and to fix them if they arise). Sometimes empirical tests reveal
> that the planned reform will indeed work – but that some variation on
> it, or some alternative, will work even better. Experimentation, with care-
> ful controls, is a primary goal of the nudge enterprise. Fortunately, many
> nudge-type experiments can be run rapidly and at low cost, and in a fashion
> that allows for continuous measurement and improvement. The reason is

that such experiments sometimes involve small changes to existing programs, and those changes can be incorporated into current initiatives with relatively little expense or effort.

It is interesting to note the approach taken by the Singapore government. Singapore's policymakers understand that the governmental solutions they introduce might not work satisfactorily from the start. In their view, "finding the right policy design is . . . a process of experimentation, error and learning-by-doing" (Low 2012, p. 7).

Nudging around the world

The publication of Richard Thaler and Cass Sunstein's *Nudge* (2009) book created a lot of excitement in some quarters. It did not take long for the authors to be sought out by a number of government leaders who were interested in utilizing the nudge concept. Thaler, for instance, was contacted by several leaders in the UK Conservative Party. For more on this, consult Chapter 33 in Thaler's (2015) *Misbehaving* book. These UK government leaders were quick to understand the potential of nudging, and they established a Behavioural Insights Team (BIT). The official mission of the BIT was "to spread understanding of behavioral approaches across government and to achieve at least a tenfold return on the cost of the unit. The basic idea was to use the findings of behavioral science to improve the workings of government" (p. 334). Early on, Thaler had a number of meetings with UK government leaders, usually one or more high-level government officials and the head(s) of a particular department. According to Thaler (p. 334), "we would typically begin these meetings by asking what problems the department faced and then brainstorm about what might be done to help." According to Thaler (pp. 334–343), the BIT's activities went relatively smoothly. The nudge concept was accepted and became highly influential in a relatively short time, and nudges were utilized in quite a few governmental departments. The UK BIT's initiatives were in numerous areas, including smoking cessation, energy efficiency, organ donation, consumer protection, and compliance strategies (especially related to taxation). On the other side of the Atlantic, Cass Sunstein joined the Obama Administration and served as Administrator of the U.S. White House Office of Information and Regulatory Affairs during 2009 to 2012 (Sunstein 2016, p. 46). According to Sunstein, "a number of people in the Obama Administration took the findings of BE quite seriously. We adopted a large number of initiatives that count as nudges" (p. 46). "The relevant initiatives [include] . . . disclosure, warnings, norms, and default rules, and they can be found in multiple areas, including fuel economy, energy efficiency, environmental protection, health care, and obesity" (p. 46).

> Now other countries are also joining the movement. A study conducted by the Economic and Social Research Council published in 2014 reports that 136 countries around the world have incorporated behavioral sciences in some aspects of public policy, and 51 'have developed centrally directed policy initiatives that have been influenced by the new behavioural sciences'. (Thaler 2015, p. 344)

> It is clear that behavioral findings are having a large impact on regulation, law, and public policy all over the world, and with increasing global interest in low-cost regulatory tools, that impact will inevitably grow over the next decades. (Sunstein 2016, p. 46)

Conclusion

Nudges are a liberty-preserving approach that steer people in particular directions in order to improve their well-being but also allow them to go their own way. They can be used by both private and public institutions (Sunstein 2014, pp. 583–584). Both types of institutions have shown mounting interest in the use of nudges because they generally cost little and have the potential to promote many economic and other goals. Nudges are needed because humans have limited cognitive abilities and are frequently biased in their judgments and decision making. As a result, humans often make decisions (or fail to make decisions) in a way that does not allow them to attain their potential well-being. So nudges at relatively little cost can help people's lives be healthier, happier, easier, wealthier, safer, less complex, and less of a struggle than they would otherwise be without sacrificing their freedom of choice. Nudges are designed by choice architects using knowledge of human behavior and knowledge of particular situations in which people often make poor choices. It is to be expected that all of us will benefit as more types of nudges are developed for use in more different situations in more parts of the world, and we learn how to integrate nudges with standard government regulatory practices.

NOTE

1 This is a revised and simplified example of the one that Thaler and Sunstein (2009, pp. 1–3) use to introduce the nudge concept.

References

Low, Donald (ed) 2012. *Behavioural Economics and Policy Design: Examples from Singapore*. London: World Scientific.

Sunstein, Cass R. 2014. "Nudging: A Very Short Guide," *Journal of Consumer Policy*, 37, 583–588.

Sunstein, Cass R. 2016. "Behaviorally Informed Regulation, Part 1," in Frantz, Roger, Chen, Shu-Heng, Dopfer, Kurt, Heukelom, Floris and Mousavi, Shabnam (eds) *Routledge Handbook of Behavioural Economics*. New York: Routledge, 45–59.

Thaler, Richard H. 2015. *Misbehaving: The Making of Behavioral Economics*. New York: Norton.

Thaler, Richard H. and Benartzi, Shlomo. 2004. "Save More Tomorrow: Using Behavioral Economics to Increase Employer Saving," *Journal of Political Economy*, 112, S164–S187.

Thaler, Richard H. and Sunstein, Cass R. 2003. "Libertarian Paternalism," *American Economic Review*, 93(2), May, 175–179.

Thaler, Richard H. and Sunstein, Cass R. 2009. *Nudge: Improving Decisions About Health, Wealth, and Happiness*. Revised and Expanded Edition. New York: Penguin Books.

Thaler, Richard H., Sunstein, Cass R. and Balz, John p. 2013. "Choice Architecture," in Shafir, Eldar (ed) *The Behavioral Foundations of Public Policy*. Princeton: Princeton University Press, 428–439.

Tomer, John F. 2013. "Stemming the Tide of Obesity: What Needs to Happen," *Journal of Socio-Economics*, 42, 88–98.

United Kingdom, House of Lords, Science and Technology Select Committee. 2011. "Behaviour Change: Report," 2nd Report of Session 2010–2012, London: The Stationery Office Limited.

8 Law and behavioral economics

Recall in chapter 2 that BE emerged as heterodox economists became very critical of the scientific methods of neoclassical economics (NE). In particular, these economists were very critical of the rational choice theory of NE in which the economic actors were depicted as ruthless self-interested maximizers of their well-being. Behaviorally oriented economists were also very critical at that time of the narrowness of NE, notably its lack of connection with psychology and other social sciences, not to mention its excessive reliance on mathematics. As indicated in the following sections of this chapter, many legal scholars ultimately became similarly disenchanted with NE.

Law and economics

By the early 1980s, if not before, legal scholars were coming to recognize that the law is in a sense a behavioral system. It is a system that "seeks to shape behavior – to regulate, to incentivize, to nudge people to behave in some ways and not to behave in others . . . and legal scholars [were coming] to understand that human behavior can be deliberately shaped through many mechanisms beyond the administration of technically managed formal rules," notably by economic incentives, social norms, and psychological influences (Ulen 2014, p. 93). Note that "the study of law and behavior is distinctive because law seeks to intentionally shape people's behavior by reference to some measure of *social* good" (p. 94). In order for law to realize its potential as a behavioral system, law needs a behavioral theory that can explain how actors subject to the legal system will respond to different types of legal actions. That is why legal scholars in the early 1980s decided to link law with economics. The area known as law and economics came into existence as legal scholars imported from mainstream economics a series of assumptions about how people respond to different situations. The assumptions they imported were essentially those of rational choice theory in which individuals were assumed to choose actions that maximized their well-being or, in the case of businesses, their profit. Gradually, the law and economics discipline progressed as the tools of NE were adapted in order to understand people's behavior with respect to the law (Korobkin and Ulen 2000, p. 1055). Two important legal insights stemmed from the assumption that people respond rationally to incentives. "First, the law can serve as a powerful tool to encourage socially desirable conduct and discourage undesirable conduct. In the hands of skillful policymakers, the law can be used to subsidize some behaviors and to tax others" (p. 1054). Second, the law, intentionally or intentionally, can encourage the efficient use of resources, can encourage production, or can encourage redistribution of resource ownership (p. 1054).

As law and economics "reached intellectual maturity" in the early 2000s, many lawyers were coming to appreciate that the rationality assumptions were severely limiting law and economics' continued scholarly development (Korobkin and Ulen 2000, p. 1055). "There is simply too much credible experimental evidence that individuals frequently act in ways that are incompatible with the assumptions of rational choice theory" (p. 1055). Further, many lawyers who had analysed the incentive effects of laws based on the implausible rationality assumptions began to realize that the result cannot possibly be efficacious legal policy (pp. 1055–1056). Consequently, much effort has been devoted to understanding the deficiencies of mainstream law and economics. The following sections outline a number of the problematic aspects associated with law and economics and explain the kind of economics that law needs to be paired with.

Before turning to the problematic aspects of law and economics, let's consider a few of its beneficial aspects. According to NE, a key part of law and economics, when people who are behaving in a rational manner freely engage in market exchange, the market outcomes will be optimal for all participants in the sense that all will be better off, and the overall outcome will be characterized by an efficient use of resources. Note as well that according to NE theory, there are a significant number of situations in which the optimal outcomes will be precluded due to "market failures." Because of market failures, the voluntary choices of rational, self-interested individuals will lead to collectively suboptimal outcomes. In other words, in these cases there is a "disjunction between what is individually rational and what is collectively rational" (Ulen 1994, p. 492). Four types of market failure are notable: 1) public goods, 2) external costs or benefits, 3) imperfect competition (where market power is present), and 4) severe informational asymmetry (pp. 492–493).

Consider the public good case of market failure. Public goods are collectively consumed, and consumers cannot be excluded from consuming the good if they do not pay for it (Ulen 1994, pp. 492–493). A fireworks display and national defense are examples of public goods. The market for public goods fails because consumers have a strong incentive to free ride, and thus, businesses will not be able to profit from supplying the good. As a result, little or none of the good can be expected to be produced (a suboptimal outcome). Because free market exchange fails to produce the good, supply by the government (or some other non-market solution) will be necessary, assuming the benefits of the good, if produced, would substantially exceed its costs.

Consider the typical case of market failure due to external costs: businesses in the process of producing their goods impose harmful costs on others, costs that they do not incur. One example is the business that imposes costs on others by polluting the air in a way that contributes to local residents' respiratory problems and adversely affects the exteriors of residents' houses. As a consequence, the market is said to fail in that a suboptimally large amount of the company's goods are supplied, and the welfare of those who experience costly harms is reduced. According to NE, the classic solution to this problem is to penalize the business by an amount that equals the harmful cost that they have imposed on others. This "solution" to the market failure would in theory result in both an optimal amount of production and an improvement of the welfare of those who were harmed. In a similar fashion, for the imperfect competition case in which there is a monopoly firm or a number of near monopoly firms, NE theory explains why the market fails to produce an optimal, welfare-maximizing amount of goods. NE theory also provides an analysis of the severe informational asymmetry case and recommends a solution to the associated market failure.

The above theory, which is part of law and economics, is important because it outlines where voluntary market exchange is expected to perform satisfactorily and where it is not expected to perform well. Thus, law and economics have implications for how the law should be structured to encourage efficient resource use. The key questions are: When should voluntary exchange be encouraged? And when will other forms of economic organization be necessary and need encouragement? (Ulen 1994, p. 515). No doubt, the NE theory that deals with market failure has an economic logic to it and makes some sense. Nevertheless, there are many reasons why NE theory fails to appreciate the way that people and businesses typically behave. As Jolls, Sunstein and Thaler (1998, pp. 1476–1479) have explained in their very influential paper, rather than attempting to maximize their well-being by behaving in a hyper rational manner, individuals' behavior typically manifests bounded rationality, bounded self-interest, and bounded willpower. Similarly, while interested in profits, businesses are typically not hyper rational in their focus on profitability. As legal scholars have come to understand these weaknesses of law and economics, they have sought an alternative approach. The alternative approach has taken on a couple of different labels. Some groups of legal scholars call the alternative approach law and socio-economics; others call it law and behavioral economics or even law and behavioral science. These different labels reflect to some degree differences among legal scholars in their understandings of what the legal profession needs and what law and economics fails to provide.

Law and socio-economics

According to Robert Ashford, lawyers would be much better off if they endorsed law and socio-economics rather than law and economics. Let's first consider the essential nature of socio-economics. "Socio-economics is a positive and normative approach that aspires to present a factually rigorous, holistic understanding of economic phenomena" (Ashford 2007, p. 1405). Socio-economics does not subscribe to rational choice theory. Correspondingly, socio-economists recognize that humans are not simply self-interested, but that humans are also interested in the well-being of others. Socio-economics is firmly based on the use of scientific methods, both with regard to empirical and theoretical research. Socio-economics "does not require the adoption of any particular school of economic thought" (p. 1406). Unlike NE, socio-economics is very much a multi-disciplinary approach. It encompasses economics, psychology, sociology, political science, biology, anthropology, philosophy, history, law, and management (Harrison 1999, p. 225). While recognizing the powerful and pervasive influence of NE, socio-economists seek to understand the limitations of NE, improve on it, and develop alternatives to it (Ashford 2005, p. 1). Moreover, socio-economics recognizes that "individual choices are shaped not only by notions of rationality and self-interest but also by emotions, social bonds, beliefs, expectations, and a sense of morality" (p. 2). In other words, socio-economics considers the whole person.[1]

Jeffrey Harrison (1999, p. 224) argues that "the fit is better between law and socio-economics than it is between law and economics; in other words, socio-economics is the better complement to law." The most important reason for this is that socio-economics is superior to economics in its understanding of what is just. From the standpoint of NE, a just outcome occurs when a reallocation of resources leaves at least one person better off and no one worse off (p. 225). As the above indicates, the emphasis in standard economics is on market exchanges that make people better or worse off in a material sense; it is also on what may make them feel better or worse (p. 226). So, if in an exchange between two parties, each party winds up better off (or at least not worse off) in both material and feeling senses, then the outcome would be considered just. From a socio-economic standpoint, on the other hand, things are less straightforward. To understand justice from a socio-economic point of view requires attention to the social interactions involved and individuals' psychological characteristics (p. 230). To fully appreciate whether justice has been done, one needs to know how people assess the gains and/or losses involved. In socio-economics, justice is a multidimensional concept; it is not merely related to material considerations. Recall that ideally what a legal system needs are "laws designed to encourage people to do what is 'right'." For this to happen, it is necessary that the legal system embody a "broad understanding of the motivational dimensions of human beings" (p. 231). Justice requires that legal decisions recognize "the obligations people feel to each other and the extent to which they act from a sense of duty" (p. 231). The upshot is that with respect to justice, the breadth of law and socio-economics makes it far superior to the narrowness of law and economics.

Robert Ashford also believes that socio-economics is a better fit for law than standard economics. His argument is based on understanding the proper role of the good lawyer in the American legal system. As he points out, the role of a lawyer is governed by rules of professional responsibility. The good lawyer is a "guardian of [his clients'] personal and property rights within an adversary system" (Ashford 1997, p. 2).

> Lawyers are required to determine client objectives, get the facts straight, understand the practical limitations of evidence, know the law, serve clients competently within the bounds of the law and improve the legal system for clients and society. (Ashford 1997, p. 3)

A good lawyer is not wedded to a single discipline. Rather, she draws from all relevant disciplines to help inform her decisions. Good lawyers are sensitive to the effect of values, morality, emotions, beliefs, expectations and irrationality on the economic behavior of clients, adversaries, third parties, lawyers and judges. The good lawyer assumes people are not atomistic, one-dimensional profit maximizers. Instead, she realizes people are inextricably connected to others in a way that cannot be fully explained or predicted by a one-dimensional utility function, no matter how broadly conceived. (Ashford 1997, p. 3)

Clearly, a lawyer wedded to the narrow perspectives of law and economics (and therefore NE) cannot be a good lawyer in the view articulated by Ashford. Socio-economics has the broad perspective that is needed to be compatible with the broad responsibilities expected to be carried out by good lawyers.

Socio-economics compared to behavioral economics

One might ask: How does socio-economics compare with BE? Socio-economics, compared to BE, is a broader, less distinct subject area that owes a great deal to BE research. Both socio-economic and BE scholars are opposed to the scientific methods that are most characteristic of NE. That is, they are opposed to rational choice theory, opposed to positivistic scientific methods, opposed to the rigidity and narrowness of NE, opposed to the excessive use of mathematics, and in favor of making economics an interdisciplinary social science (Chapter 2). One problem with comparing BE with socio-economics is that BE has a number of strands. One very important and prominent strand is psychological economics that derives from the work of psychologists Kahneman and Tversky. As indicated in Chapter 2, their research focuses a great deal on the cognitive functioning of humans and why people are prone to making predictable errors in their judgments and decision making. Consider Matthew Rabin, a psychological economic practitioner, whose research is similar to other behavioral economists in this field. Compared to NE, his research incorporates much greater psychological realism, utilizes mathematics to a lesser extent, and makes less use of positivist methods; nevertheless he utilizes many of the methods and assumptions of NE (Chapter 2). Because of this, some socio-economic scholars have not accepted the term BE even though they draw on a good deal of BE thought to explain why they reject NE. In essence, socio-economics is a broader, more diffuse, and more interdisciplinary version of BE.

Law and behavioral economics (or socio-economics)

As indicated earlier, law combined with NE, also known as law and economics, made an important contribution in that it enabled legal scholars to understand how laws should be structured to overcome market failures and, thereby, contribute to economic efficiency. For example, law and economics outlined how law should deal with market failures in the cases of public goods, external costs and benefits, and excessive market power. In spite of this contribution, law and economics has suffered from its problematic assumption of perfect human rationality, an assumption that is quite obviously not realistic. To correct this problem, a great many legal scholars have turned to law and behavioral economics (or law and socio-economics), because both of these areas "build on the core insights of law and economics scholarship but take seriously the shortcomings of rational choice theory" (Korobkin and Ulen 2000, p. 1057). Both subject areas utilize the important insights of BE, especially the insights of psychological economics and those stemming from the bounded rationality research of Herbert Simon. The goal of law and BE (or socio-economics) is to create laws that embody behavioral realism, and therefore, help to create a legal system with the desired incentive effects (p. 1058). As a result of the integration of law with BE, law now better reflects the view that people typically make decisions whose outcomes fall far short of economic optimality (p. 1143). One example is that laws may embody the insight that people's decision making behavior depends on in a decision context, i.e., that "situational variables are critical inputs into decision making" (p. 1143). Second, contrary to rational choice theory, law and BE increasingly reflects the observation that people typically do not behave in a strictly selfish manner. For example, people in their decision making generally consider the fairness of an action, consider the needs of their community, and engage in considerable cooperation. People also often voluntarily contribute to the provision of public goods. Thus, the perspective of law and BE is that people are not unboundedly rational and unboundedly self-interested. People deviate from the strict economic rationality of NE. These deviations, however, may in many cases be properly understood as the sensible and understandable behavior of humans (p. 1144).

Not surprisingly in other cases, people who act in an economically irrational manner may fail to do what is in their best interests. Because of this, there may be a need for laws with some degree of paternalism that provide helpful inducements to people, thereby enabling them to achieve their desired ends. This might involve either deterring socially undesirable behavior or encouraging desirable behaviors that tend to enhance human health and well-being (Jolls, Sunstein, and Thaler 1998, p. 1522). Such laws could encourage desired behavior by reframing the situation, or making desired choices vivid and salient, or counteracting people's tendency for over-optimism. Or laws might make helpful nudges possible (pp. 1536–1537). Laws can also help deal with "criminals" who are likely to lack self-control. Some criminal behavior can be deterred by raising the actual or perceived costs of criminal acts or, given that law breakers tend to discount the future heavily, criminals might be deterred by influencing the timing of costs and penalties incurred by them (pp. 1538–1539). Another area where law might be involved is related to people's typical decision making errors and their judgment biases. These cognitive shortcomings create opportunities for opportunistic marketers who may be able to take advantage of their customers' shortcomings using false and misleading claims about their products' qualities or availability (Zamir 2016, pp. 5–6). Note that there is a kind of "market failure" in the situations mentioned above. The market failure, however, is very different from the type of failure mentioned earlier in which the failure stemmed from the structure of the market. In the failure situations mentioned above, the failure is related to humans' cognitive functioning particularly with respect to decision making (Ulen 1994, p. 521). Because the two types of market failure are quite different, they call for very different legal remedies.

In sum, using BE, the law can come to embody many novel prescriptions regarding how to make the legal system work better (Jolls, Sunstein and Thaler, p. 1546). And using BE, the law can come to better indicate when paternalism is appropriate and what kinds of paternalism are most appropriate.

NOTE

1 The Socio-Economic Section of the Association of American Law Schools is an important meeting ground for those interested in law and socio-economics.

References

Ashford, Robert.1997. "Socio-Economics: What Is Its Place in Law Practice," *Wisconsin Law Review*, 611, 1–9.

Ashford, Robert. 2005. "Socio-Economics – An Overview," July 4, Available at SSRN. 1–6.

Ashford, Robert. 2007. "Socioeconomics," in Clark, David S. (ed) *Encyclopedia of Law and Society: American and Global Perspectives*. Los Angeles: Sage Publications, 1405–1408.

Harrison, Jeffrey L. 1999. "Law and Socioeconomics," *Journal of Legal Education*, 49(2), June, 224–235.

Jolls, Christine; Sunstein, Cass and Thaler, Richard H. 1998. "A Behavioral Approach to Law and Economics," *Stanford Law Review*, 50(5), May, 1471–1550.

Korobkin, Russell B. and Ulen, Thomas S. 2000. "Law and Behavioral Science: Removing the Rationality Assumption from Law and Economics," *California Law Review*, 88(4), July, 1051–1144.

Ulen, Thomas S. 1994. "Rational Choice and the Economic Analysis of Law," *Law and Social Inquiry*, 19(2), Spring, 487–522.

Ulen, Thomas S. 2014. "The Importance of Behavioral Law," in Zamir, Eyal and Teichman, Doron (eds) *The Oxford Handbook of Behavioral Economics and the Law*. Oxford: Oxford University Press, 93–124.

Zamir, Eyal. 2016. "Law and Behavioral Economics," in *Encyclopedia of the Philosophy of Law and Social Philosophy* (Forthcoming). Available at SSRN. May 8, 1–10.

9 Behavioral macroeconomics

Keynesian macroeconomics

In order to understand behavioral macroeconomics, it is necessary to start at the beginning of modern macroeconomics. That is, we need to start in 1936 with the publication of John Maynard Keynes' *General Theory*. The macroeconomics that Keynes created is focused on the problem of depression or recession. More particularly, it is concerned with why a nation's output might become substantially lower than its potential output or why a nation's unemployment rate might become substantially higher than the unemployment rate associated with full employment. The solution for a depressed economy that follows from Keynes' theoretical framework is to use activist monetary and fiscal policy to raise the nation's aggregate demand. When aggregate demand rises and becomes higher than current output, businesses can be expected to respond by supplying more goods to the market. Because of the greater production, businesses can be expected to hire more employees, thereby raising employment and lowering unemployment. On the other hand, if for some reason aggregate demand falls significantly, the process is expected to work in reverse as businesses supply fewer goods, and the lower output leads them to lay off employees. In the case of such a downturn, will not the natural working of market processes spontaneously lead to a recovery? In Keynes' view, there are obstacles in the way of an economy automatically bouncing back when unemployment becomes excessive. One such obstacle is that wages and prices tend to be "sticky" in the downward direction. In a downturn, rigid wage rates, for example, ones that do not naturally decline, means the value of the hourly wage rate will become higher than the value of the output that the worker can produce in that hour. And that means that businesses will have no incentive to hire workers or retain workers when demand falls. As a consequence, there is no automatic tendency for the unemployment rate to bounce back. Further, Keynes' analysis of depression included a variety of non-rational behaviors of important economic actors.

Macroeconomic evolution

In addition to understanding the basic elements of Keynesian macroeconomics, it is important to have an appreciation of how modern macroeconomics has evolved over the last 75 years or so. In the 1940s and 1950s, Keynesian economics gradually gained adherents especially among younger economists, and these economists in a variety of ways began translating Keynesian concepts into mathematics, graphs, and equilibrium models. By the late 1960s, there was a great deal of agreement regarding the content of Keynesian macroeconomics and on its usefulness in both explaining macroeconomic fluctuations and for providing useful policy guidance (see Akerlof 2007, p. 5). At this time, Keynesian macroeconomics was called the neoclassical synthesis; it included a fixed money wage and equilibrium analysis (Akerlof 2002, p. 411). Gradually, this version of Keynesian macroeconomics evolved into New Keynesian macroeconomics. New Keynesians "continued to believe in an active role for the government. Yet ... they mostly accepted the notion that investors and consumers are rational and that markets generally get it right" (Krugman 2009, p. 5). It was Keynesian, but it departed significantly from Keynes' thinking. It should be noted that to make their macroeconomic theory more realistic and more Keynesian, New Keynesians added a variety of "frictions" including credit constraints, market imperfections, information failures, tax distortions, staggered contracts, uncertainty, menu costs, and bounded rationality (Akerlof 2007, p. 6).

In the late 1960s and early 1970s, New Classical (NC) economics emerged. NC economists "completely rejected Keynes's framework for understanding economic slumps" (Krugman 2009, p. 5). The emergence of NC economics was an anti-Keynesian counterrevolution. In other words, NC economics involved a full scale "retreat from Keynesianism and a return to neoclassism" (p. 4). NC economists had a strong belief in the free market and that free market economies would never go astray (p. 2). In other words, they believed that free market economies have an automatic tendency to bounce back from economic downturns. Moreover, NC economists "saw the ... weaknesses in the micro foundations of [Keynesian] macroeconomics ...; they hated its lack of rigor" (Akerof 2002, p. 411). In NC theorizing, the decisions of all economic actors are consistent with rational, maximizing behavior, and NC economists rejected the assumption of sticky money wages (p. 412). According to Krugman's (2009, p. 2) critical characterization, "as memories of the Depression faded, [NC] economists fell back in love with the old, idealized vision of an economy in which rational individuals interact in perfect markets, this time gussied up with fancy equations." "By 1975, economists had divided into [two] opposing camps," Keynesians and the New Classicals (the anti-Keynesian neoclassical economists) (p. 8). In contrast to Keynesians, NC economists believe that "a general lack of sufficient demand isn't possible, because prices always move to match supply with demand" (p. 9). Consequently, NC economists see little or no need for activist countercyclical policies. NC economists also do not agree with the Keynesian description of workers who are unable to find a job as being involuntarily unemployed. In the NC view, workers seeking employment should always be considered voluntarily unemployed. Such workers in their view are simply rejecting available jobs because the pay and conditions of work for these jobs are not satisfactory (Akerlof 2002, p. 414).

Toward a behavioral macroeconomics

George Akerlof has been the most important contributor to the development of behavioral macroeconomics. His "dream was to develop . . . a behavioral macroeconomics in the original spirit of John Maynard Keynes' *General Theory*" (Akerlof 2002, p. 411). He sought to develop a macroeconomics that was consistent with Keynes' original contribution, but unlike New Keynesian macroeconomics. He was certainly not interested in a macroeconomics based on neoclassical behavioral assumptions. What Akerlof has done is to strengthen macroeconomic theory by incorporating assumptions based on sound psychology and sociology (p. 411). Accordingly, his research has utilized behavioral science concepts such as cognitive bias, reciprocity, fairness, herding, social status, and other similar concepts used by behavioral economists. Akerlof's orientation has been to create models that "are constructed with careful attention to realistic microeconomic detail" (p. 414).

One of Akerlof's most important contributions is the concept of efficiency wages. Akerlof and a number of his collaborators, including his wife Janet Yellen, have developed efficiency wage theories to explain the existence of involuntary unemployment. Efficiency wage models "posit that, for reasons such as morale, fairness, insider power, or asymmetric information, employers have strong motives to pay workers more than the minimum necessary to attract them" (Akerlof 2002, p. 414). When a company pays wages above the market clearing wage, the employer will have more job applicants than they wish to hire. In this situation, the employer will typically ration the jobs, offering employment to only a fraction of the applicants. The workers who are seeking but unable to find employment are involuntarily unemployed. The degree to which efficiency wages exceed the market clearing wage tends to be different in different sectors of the economy, which leads to a "dispersion in earnings across seemingly similar jobs and among workers with apparently identical characteristics" (pp. 414–415). Further, it is interesting to note that, other things being the same, industries with higher pay typically have lower quit rates and better working conditions compared to industries with lower pay (p. 415). Thus, there are "good jobs" and "bad jobs." And workers can be involuntarily unemployed not simply because of companies' practice of paying efficiency wage rates but also because some companies have a practice of offering good jobs and other companies do not.

Let's consider more fully the psychological and sociological reasons why firms pay efficiency wages. One explanation is reciprocity or gift exchange. If employers give workers a higher wage than is necessary to hire them, workers tend to reciprocate this "gift" and make a greater commitment to the firm than if they had only been paid the minimum necessary wage (Akerlof 2002, p. 415). Similarly, a firm that pays its workers an above-market clearing wage may avoid worker perceptions that their wages are unfair. Workers tend to exert less effort when they perceive that their employers are treating them unfairly (p. 415). Note that group norms governing the workplace are very important in determining how workers perceive the fairness and "gifts" of their employers. More generally, norms are important in many contexts as they "reflect how . . . [different] decision makers think they and others *should* or *should not* behave" (Akerlof 2007, p. 6). Considering norms takes into account the purposefulness of human decision making (p. 31). An interesting version of efficiency wage theory is the insider-outsider model, "whereby insider workers prevent the firm from hiring outsiders at a . . . wage lower than what the insiders are currently receiving. This theory implicitly assumes that insiders have the ability to sabotage the inclusion of new workers into a firm" (Akerlof 2002, p. 415). Another version of efficiency wage theory views above-market clearing wages as a disciplinary device. In this model, "firms pay 'high' wages to reduce the incentive of workers to shirk. The attempt of all firms to pay 'above-average' wages . . . pushes the average level of wages above market clearing, creating unemployment. Unemployment serves as a disciplinary device, because workers who are caught shirking and fired for lack of effort can become reemployed only after a period of unemployment" (pp. 415–416).

Besides Akerlof's theory that firms pay workers efficiency wages, there is another important element to Akerlof 's understanding of wage rates. Akerlof (2002, p. 420) agrees with Keynes that "workers resist, and firms rarely impose, cuts in nominal pay." Keynes' assumption about workers' resistance to nominal wage cuts was based on his intuitive understanding of psychology (p. 420). According to Akerlof, this worker resistance to cutting wages is consistent with theory and evidence deriving from prospect theory. "Prospect theory posits that individuals evaluate changes in their circumstances according to the gains or losses they entail relative to some reference point. [As indicated in an earlier chapter,] the evidence suggests that individuals place much greater weight on avoiding losses than on incurring gains . . . . Downward wage rigidity is a natural implication of prospect theory if the current money wage is taken as a reference point by workers in measuring gains and losses" (p. 420). Workers like most other people are loss averse.[1]

Truman Bewley (1999) addressed the question of why wages do not fall during a recession. To find the answer, he interviewed 336 managers, labor leaders, and employment counselors in Connecticut and nearby states (Howitt 2002, p. 126). From the interviewees' responses, he found that an important part of the answer is that employers value good morale among their firm's workforce:

> Good morale . . . has a positive effect on the firm's profits by increasing the workers' productivity, effort, creativity, and cooperativeness, and by reducing absenteeism and turnover; well-motivated employees also tend to provide good customer service, giving the firm a good reputation. However, morale is fragile and will deteriorate quickly if workers feel they are being slighted or treated unfairly or if, for whatever reason, they cease to identify with the goals of their organization. (p. 126)

Accordingly, employers are reluctant to cut workers' nominal wage because they know workers would interpret such a cut as an unfair, hostile act, which would lower their morale (p. 126). Bewley's interviews were done in person in great depth. From these interviews, it was very clear that "managers see morale as the overriding factor in determining the success of their employee relations" (p. 128). Bewley found that of the 55 employers that did cut wages, 51 percent said that this led to serious morale problems (p. 129). Using data from individual firms' records, Bewley also found that "nominal wage cuts are indeed rare and that when they take place they are almost always associated with some unusual circumstances" (p. 130). These findings are consistent with reciprocity theory in that "people [say, workers] will spend considerable resources to punish others [say, employers] for what they perceive as hostile acts" (p. 134). Further, these findings are consistent with behavioral science, but they are totally inconsistent with traditional economic maximizing behavior. Bewley's work is significant because it provides a close-up view of actual labor market behavior, and it raises the prospect that behavioral macroeconomics might become more empirically oriented (p. 137).

Animal spirits and the macroeconomy

According to George Akerlof and Robert Shiller (2009), understanding the behavior of the macroeconomy has two main parts. The first part deals with the logic of decision making and relationships. This part consists of the relatively straightforward, standard analyses of economic and financial behavior carried out by macroeconomists, whether Keynesian or non-Keynesian. The second part, however, explains the part of macroeconomic behavior that to a considerable extent defies understanding by those whose expertise consists only in the standard economic and financial disciplines. Keynes had some understanding of this second part; he used the term "animal spirits" to refer to this behavior. In their book, *Animal Spirits: How Human Psychology Drives the Economy and Why It Matters for Global Capitalism*, Akerlof and Shiller (2009) have explained the role that humans' animal spirits play in contributing to the ups and downs of capitalist economies and how this aspect differs from the phenomena that more traditional economic analyses focus on. Note that Akerlof and Shiller's concept of animal spirits is akin to Keynes' concept but is more elaborated and different in some of its specific aspects.

In general, animal spirits refer to a restless, inconsistent, uncertain element in the economy (Akerlof and Shiller 2009, p. 4). According to Akerlof and Shiller (p. ix), there are five psychological factors that constitute the essential elements of animal spirits. These are confidence, fairness, corruption and bad faith, money illusion, and stories. In other words, due to people's animal spirits, they are very influenced by 1) whether they are treated fairly, 2) their vulnerability to the temptations of corruption, 3) their repulsion from evil deeds, 4) their confusion due to inflation, and 5) they are influenced by stories more than by economic reasoning (p. 73). Changes related to these factors are the ultimate reason for most booms and busts, and this is certainly true of the boom and the bust that occurred in the first decade of the twenty-first century. "These phenomena cannot be understood in terms of traditional economic theory alone" (p. ix).

The stories we create and tell ourselves and others about the economy are arguably the most important aspect of animal spirits. Stories are important because "the human mind is built to think in terms of narratives, of sequences of events with an internal logic and dynamic that appear as a unified whole" (Akerlof and Shiller 2009, p. 51). Human motivation derives from the stories we tell ourselves. Also, "people's memories of essential facts are . . . indexed in the brain around stories" (p. 51). When many people in a nation or region share common stories, it is possible for their stories to move markets and the economy (p. 54). Stories related to high confidence such as inspirational stories about new businesses or new types of businesses (new era stories) or tales of how some people ingeniously are getting rich have been associated with major booms in economies around the world (p. 55). These kinds of confidence inducing, inspirational stories can spread contagiously and reach epidemic proportions, even becoming manias, or panics in the case of declining confidence (p. 56). Such stories urge people to act spontaneously and involve a kind of motivation very different from that associated with economic rationality (p. 3).

The essential thing to understand about animal spirits is that these non-economic, largely non-rational motives govern a great deal of economic activity. "In Keynes' view these animal spirits are the main cause for why the economy fluctuates as it does. They are also the main cause of involuntary unemployment" (Akerlof and Shiller 2009, p. xxiii). This brings us to the role of government. According to Akerlof and Shiller (and Keynes):

> capitalist societies . . . can be tremendously creative. Government should interfere as little as possible with that creativity. On the other hand, *left to their own devices*, capitalist economies will pursue excess . . . . There will be *manias*. The manias will be followed by *panics*. There will be joblessness. People will consume too much and save too little. Minorities will be mistreated and will suffer. House prices, stock prices, and the price of oil will boom and then bust. The proper role of the government, like the proper

role of the ... parent, is to set the stage. The stage should give full rein to the creativity of capitalism. But it should also countervail the excesses that occur because of our animal spirits. (Akerlof and Shiller 2009, pp. xxiii–xxiv)

In other words, government should not be overly permissive. Government should recognize that people are human, have animal spirits, and accordingly, an economy needs both activist policy and a significant amount of regulation to control and counter the excesses (p. xxiv).

Discussion

Behavioral economics (BE) has not had the impact on macroeconomics that BE has had in the microeconomic area (Thaler 2015, p. 349). According to Thaler (p. 350), there are a few reasons for this. First, "the field lacks the two key ingredients that contributed to the success of behavioral finance: 1) the theories do not make easily falsifiable predictions and 2) the data are relatively scarce" (pp. 349–350). Another difficulty is that the two main groups of macroeconomists, Keynesians and non-Keynesians, have strong opinions and seem unable to agree on even the most basic advice about what to do during a recession (p. 350). Nevertheless, it is clear to me and like-minded others such as Paul Krugman that a behaviorally realistic macroeconomics would need to follow the path of Akerlof and Shiller and be in the Keynesian tradition. As Krugman (2009, p. 2) has indicated, what is not needed in macroeconomics are more impressive, intellectually elegant, neoclassical mathematical models. "Economists need to abandon the neat but wrong solution of assuming that everyone is rational and that markets work perfectly" (p. 19). Clearly, "Keynesian economics remains the best framework we have for making sense of recessions and depressions" (p. 18). There does seem to be substantial scope for building on the behavioral macroeconomic contributions of Akerlof and others, and thereby, improving behavioral macroeconomics and making it an area that politicians and the public can increasingly rely on to deal with the problems of recession and inflation.[2] [3]

NOTES

1 Contrary to the wisdom of Akerlof and other Keynesians such as Samuelson and Krugman, Paul Davidson, a leading Keynesian macroeconomist, does not agree that the rigidity of money wages is the essential reason for the tendency of capitalist economies to periodically fall into recession/depression. In Davidson's (2016) view, it is the essential properties of liquid assets in the context of uncertainty that is at the heart of the problem.

2   According to John King (2013, p. 4), "there are substantial unexploited opportunities in the largely
      unexplored border terrain between behavioural economics and post-Keynesian macroeconom-
      ics." King, however, admits that "most post-Keynesians have made little or no reference to, or
      use of, behavioural economics, at least in that part of their work published in the *Journal of Post
      Keynesian Economics*" (p. 4). King notes that Paul Davidson, a prominent Post Keynesian, is inter-
      ested in BE and wrote an article entitled "Was Keynes the First Behavioural Economist?" (p. 4).
3   "Over the past 20 years, researchers have incorporated an increasing number of results from BE
      into macroeconomics models" (Driscoll and Holden 2014, p. 133). "There are many potential
      results from behavioral psychology that can be applied to macroeconomics" (p. 143).

References

Akerlof, George A. 2002. "Behavioral Macroeconomics and Macroeconomic Behavior,"
      American Economic Review, 92(3), June, 411–433.

Akerlof, George A. 2007. "The Missing Motivation in Macroeconomics," *American
      Economic Review*, 97(1), 3–36.

Akerlof, George A. and Shiller, Robert J. 2009. *Animal Spirits: How Human Psychology
      Drives the Economy, and Why It Matters for Global Capitalism*. Princeton: Princeton
      University Press.

Bewley, Truman F. 1999. *Why Wages Don't Fall During a Recession*. Cambridge, MA:
      Harvard University Press.

Davidson, Paul. 2016. "Why Neither Samuelson's Neoclassical Synthesis Keynesianism
      Nor New Keynesianism Theory is Compatible with Keynes's General Theory
      Explanation of the Cause of Unemployment," Unpublished paper presented on
      September 17 at the Post-Keynesian Conference, Kansas City.

Driscoll, John C. and Holden, Steinar. 2014. "Behavioral Economics and Macroeconomic
      Models," *Journal of Macroeconomics*, 41, 133–147.

Howitt, Peter. 2002. "Looking Inside the Labor Market: A Review Article," *Journal of
      Economic Literature*, 40, March, 125–138.

Keynes, John Maynard. 1964 [1936]. *The General Theory of Employment, Interest, and
      Money*. New York: Harcourt, Brace, and World.

King, John E. 2013. "Should Post-Keynesians Make a Behavioral Turn?" *European
      Journal of Economics and Economic Policies: Intervention*, Edward Elgar Online.

Krugman, Paul. 2009. "How Did Economists Get It So Wrong," *New York Times
      Magazine*, September 2, 1–19.

Thaler, Richard H. 2015. *Misbehaving: The Making of Behavioral Economics*. New York:
      Norton.

10 The empirical methods of behavioral economics

With regard to empirical investigation, neoclassical economics, and behavioral economics are very different

As explained in Chapter 2, neoclassical economics (NE) emphasizes the use of deductive reasoning, highly mathematical analyses, and the use of formal mathematical models that are often sophisticated and elegant. Accordingly, NE tends to put correspondingly less emphasis on empirical investigation and the use of inductive methods. Recall also that NE lacks a disciplinary connection to psychology and other social sciences. In sharp contrast to NE, behavioral economists have been critical of NE's emphasis on positivistic methods, especially their use of highly mathematical deductive analyses. And behavioral economics (BE) has emphasized interdisciplinary social science. Because, unlike NE, non-economic social science disciplines, notably psychology, put relatively greater emphasis on empirical investigation and inductive methods, so it is not surprising that behavioral economists have done likewise. Behavioral economists have also been highly motivated to use empirical methods because they have sought to disprove core NE assumptions such as that humans behave like rational economic men. More generally, as this chapter will indicate, behavioral economists are increasingly using a variety of types of empirical research in order to improve the realism of economic theory.

Experimentation in economics

It is important to note that way before both NE and BE came into existence, the view that economics was a non-experimental science was entrenched. Economic researchers believed that controlled experimentation had little to offer. For example, in 1836, John Stuart Mill said that in moral sciences such as economics, as distinguished from physical sciences, "it is seldom in our power to make experiments in them" (as quoted in Guala 2005, p. 2). This is because of "the impossibility of controlling key economic variables and of keeping background conditions fixed so that the effect of manipulating each cause in isolation can be checked" (Guala 2010, p. 99). In Mill's (and many other economists') view, this provided the main justification for economists' adoption of deductive methods that involved a mix of introspection and theoretical reasoning useful for explaining economic occurrences. Later on prominent economists such as Lionel Robbins and Milton Friedman continued to express their doubts about the possible contribution of controlled experiments (Guala 2005, p. 2). Even Paul Samuelson in the 1985 edition of his introductory text said that "economists . . . cannot perform controlled experiments . . . [Therefore] like astronomers or meteorologists they must be content largely to observe" (as quoted in Branas-Garza and Barreda 2015, p. 1). These skeptical views on economic experimentation have now largely faded away. "Economists perform hundreds of laboratory experiments every year and routinely test their theories in the laboratory [and other places]" (Guala 2005, p. 3). "Experiments are now established as a valid explanatory tool in the [economic] profession's toolkit" (Branas-Garza and Barreda 2015, pp. 1–2; Eckel 2004, p. 21). Thus, within a few decades, starting in the 1950s, economics was transformed from a non-experimental discipline to a discipline in which experimentation was an exciting and important element (Guala 2010, p. 99). Behavioral economists especially participated in and benefited from this development.

The rise of experimental economics

Why do scientists (and economists) perform experiments? Essentially economists like any other scientists want to test their theories and their understandings of principles (Smith 2000, p. 5100). They want to know if their conceptual frameworks are consistent with the kind of careful observations of economic behavior that experiments enable. They also want to know under what conditions their theories are consistent with the empirical findings. Experimentation can help economists understand the limitations of their theories. When experimental findings are at odds with accepted theory, this can lead to restructuring the theory and the development of new theories (p. 5100).

Vernon Smith is acknowledged as having laid the foundation for the field of experimental economics. For that contribution, he was awarded the Nobel Prize in 2002 (Eckel 2004, p. 15). What Smith recognized early on was that the training of economists did not lead them to think of economics "as an observational science in which the interplay between theory and observation is paramount" (Smith 1989, p. 151). In Smith's view, the purpose of theory should not just be to explain important facts; it should also be to track observations and to predict new ones (p. 152). What is desired is not simply theories with internal elegance or theories associated with authority. What we need are theories that are useful for prediction. The best theories are ones that "narrow the distance between theory and observations" (p. 152).

One important way to test economic theories is to use laboratory experiments. This involves comparing a theory's "message or its outcome implications with the experimental observations" (Smith 1994, pp. 113–114)

> Every laboratory experiment is defined by an *environment*, specifying the initial endowments, preferences and costs that motivate exchange. This environment is controlled using monetary rewards to induce the desired [participant behaviors] .... An experiment also uses an *institution* defining the language ... of market communications (bids, offers, acceptances), the rules that govern the exchange of information, and the rules [relating to making] ... contracts. This institution is defined by the experimental instructions which describe the messages and procedures of the market .... Finally, there is the observed *behavior* of the participants in the experiments. (p. 113)

Vernon Smith along with others in the field of experimental economics has typically used laboratory experiments to understand how markets work. These market related experiments enable: 1) exploring the causes of a theory's failure, 2) establishing empirical regularities as a basis for a new theory, 3) comparing how experimental outcomes change with different environments or different institutions, 4) evaluating policy proposals in light of the experimental outcomes, and 5) examining the implications of the experimental tests for new forms of exchange (Smith 1994, pp. 113–116). Often laboratory market experiments involve testing a theory's assumptions about agent behavior. Due to their design, laboratory experiments may provide outcomes that indicate whether market participants are behaving in an economically rational fashion and/or whether the process in a particular type of market is efficient. Laboratory experiments can also provide insights into whether market participants' behavior departs from narrow self-interest and instead manifests behavior that is cooperative and considerate of others.

Laboratory experiments

The key to a valuable laboratory experiment is experimental control. This involves controlling the variation of one variable, while keeping all other conditions unchanged. For example, the experiment might keep all background (environment, institution) factors constant while changing a key theoretical variable in order to test a causal hypothesis (Guala 2005, p.x). If the experimental design is effective, the background factors will be controlled. In this case, the experiment will have internal validity, which means the experiment will allow valid inferences about the effect of changing the key variable. Ideally, the experiment will also have external validity to the extent that the lab results can be generalized to the real world (p.xi). The latter will be true if the lab experiment reflects the essential features of the real world.

An important aim of running economic experiments is to understand how "normal" people function in particular situations (Branas-Garza and Barreda 2015, p.5). That is, the experiment should help us understand how people reason, learn, observe, update their beliefs, and how much time they need to do these things (p.6). Running an experiment that provides reliable and valid results is not an easy task. That is why it is important for experimenters to follow a rigorous methodology. Over the years, economic experimentalists have developed a variety of standard operating procedures and practices, and they have developed wisdom about how to run their experiments. For example, these researchers strongly hold that 1) subjects should be anonymous, 2) subjects should not be deceived, 3) subjects should receive a monetary incentive to make choices that are genuinely in their own interest, 4) subjects should face a concrete problem, 5) the experimental design needs to be clean and clear enough so that it teaches us something, and 6) the experiment should be capable of replication (pp.5–14). Several of Vernon Smith's early experiments provide good illustrations of these methods. In his experiments published in 1962 and 1964, "he showed that, when the information about the asks and bids (of sellers and buyers) was public and the agents were able to interact repeatedly in the market, both prices and quantities converged rapidly to equilibrium" (p.4).

Comparing experimental economics to behavioral economics

Although many behavioral economists have over the years come to use methods pioneered by experimental economists, it is important to take note of the differences between experimental economics (EE) and BE. EE refers primarily to a method of investigation. BE, on the other hand, is a project involving the revision of economic theory, especially the replacement of economic man with a more realistic psychological model. Behavioral economists make substantial use of experimentation but it is by no means an exclusive source of their evidence (Guala 2010, p. 104). It is important to note that in a number of ways, EE and BE have been at odds with each other. "Experimental economists [have often] conducted the same kind of experiments as the behavioral decision researchers and behavioral economists but with a different purpose" (p. 165). EE has a more pragmatic, less theoretical orientation than BE, and EE is more concerned with the behavior of markets and less concerned with the behavior of individuals. As an example of his approach to experimentation, "Smith stressed that time was necessary for the market to reach equilibrium and argued that experiments should be used to investigate which factors determine to which equilibrium the market drives the economy over time" (Heukelom 2014, p. 135). EE according to Smith has been less concerned than BE with the degree of rationality of individual market participants. One reason for this position of Smith's has been his view that "people may have very good reasons for deviating from the [rationality] axioms" (p. 136). Smith sees deviations from rationality as "not problematic because over time the market would correct those mistakes" (p. 136). Further, in Smith's view, the focus should be on the market environment that affects individual behavior (p. 137):

> In other words, EE and BE were both closely related and fundamentally different. They were closely related because they used the same set of psychological experiments to make an argument for changing the dominant neoclassical theory in economics. Furthermore, although asking different questions, they basically conducted the same experiments. They were, however, fundamentally different in the conclusions they inferred from the experimental results, . . . in the way they wanted to extend the neoclassical theory, and in the way, they considered the neoclassical theory still valuable. (Heukelom 2014, p. 168)

It should also be noted that Smith's EE and the BE deriving from Kahneman and Tversky have represented opposite sides of the political spectrum (p. 164). On the one hand, the research of EE has tended to support the conservative view that markets work quite well and converge over time to the predictions of NE. On the other hand, the research of BE has tended to support liberal views, be critical of the notion of individual rationality, and be critical of how markets work (pp. 164–165).

Beyond lab experiments: the empirical methods of behavioral economists

It is especially true in recent years that with respect to empirical methods, behavioral economists have distinguished themselves from experimental economists. Behavioral economists these days are not just using laboratory experiments; they are using a variety of empirical methods (Angner and Loewenstein 2007, p. 38). And in contrast to experimental economists, they are drawing on non-economic evidence of many kinds from a variety of disciplines. Behavioral economists also do not consider evidence from individual choices as the only kind of legitimate evidence (p. 38). Compared to experimental economists, behavioral economists are methodological eclectics who do not define themselves on the basis of the research methods they use. Although it is not unusual for behavioral economists to follow the methods of experimental economists, they have not "always endorsed all the methodological prescriptions of experimental economists" (p. 39). "Recent BE has relied on an increasingly diversified and sophisticated set of methods that reflect its interdisciplinary heritage" (p. 39).

Consider some of the non-experimental methods used by behavioral economists. First is field research using data gathered "in the field" (Angner Loewenstein 2007, p. 43). One type of field research is to use survey data that is typically gathered by administering questionnaires. The surveys might, for example, ask people not only what they did or would do in a certain situation but what was or would be their motivation. Such "surveys are straight-forward and usually yield valuable insights" (Chaudhuri 2009, p. 8). There are, however, drawbacks to this approach. The problem is that sometimes people's responses to survey questions are not entirely accurate or truthful. In other words, their responses do not always correlate well with their actual behaviors or motivations (p. 8). Another field research method involves the use of field data of various kinds. For example, in a study of the labor supply of New York City taxicab drivers, an important source of data was the "trip sheets," the "forms where drivers record the time passengers were picked up and dropped off," as well as using data on the amount of the fares from the cabs' meters (Angner and Loewenstein 2007, p. 43). It should be noted that an important reason for doing field research is the concern about the external validity of laboratory experiments. In many situations, there is good reason to think that people might make different decisions in the lab than they would make in the real world (p. 44). This might be particularly true for a question like how long or hard taxi drivers work from day to day. Of course, one of the problems with an observational field study is that it might be difficult for researchers to draw valid inferences about causation in the absence of any control over the important variables (p. 44).

Because of these concerns about internal and external validity, some behavioral economists have sought to do research using natural experiments, situations in which it might be possible to observe the causal effect of key changes in events (exogenous changes) on the variables of interest. One example of such a study involves "examining the impact of changes in defaults and other features of a company sponsored savings plan on employee savings behavior" (Angner and Loewenstein 2007, p. 45). In such a study, it can be possible to observe worker savings behavior before and after the plan change and infer that the plan change was the cause. Sometimes an actual change in nature (floods, earthquakes, etc.) might be the only important variable changing, thereby enabling researchers to treat the situation as a quasi-experiment and to draw conclusions accordingly.

In recent years, behavioral economists have begun to use field experiments; now they are the fastest growing category of empirical study. "Field experiments occupy an important middle ground between laboratory experiments and [natural experiments] . . . The underlying idea behind most field experiments is to make use of randomization in an environment that captures important characteristics of the real world" (List and Reiley 2010, p. 151). Similar to the methods often used in medical research, people are assigned at random to receive different treatments . . . including a control group that receives no treatment" (Thaler 2015, p. 338). Field experiments have external validity because they take place in situations very similar to or the same as real world conditions. They also have high internal validity because the randomized assignment to test and control groups makes it relatively easy to draw causal conclusions (Angner and Loewenstein 2007, p. 45). This is why economists refer to such field experiments as the gold standard for empirical investigation. One relatively simple example of a field experiment was the situation where "a random sample of [a company's] employees [was] . . . offered a $20 payment for attending an informational fair dealing with savings. The finding was that enrollment in the savings program was significantly higher . . . [for those] individuals [who] . . . received the monetary inducement" (p. 45). Although field experiments can have great value, it should be noted that field experiments have a variety of potential pitfalls. Typically, "such experiments are expensive and lots of stuff can go wrong" (Thaler 2015, p. 340). Unlike in lab experiments, it is difficult to detect likely problems in the setup phase, and experimenters typically cannot be present on site to deal with difficulties that arise during the experiment (p. 340).

Behavioral economists like Richard Thaler and Cass Sunstein who believe strongly in the importance of applying behavioral insights to the process of developing improved public policy also believe that such policies must be evidence based. Therefore, they have insisted that all government interventions should be tested, i.e., based on sound empirical research. Whenever possible, this testing should be field research using randomized control trials (Thaler 2015, p. 338). John List and David Reiley (2010, p. 155):

> believe that field experiments will continue to grow in popularity . . . . This growth will lead to fruitful avenues, both theoretical and empirical, but it is clear that regardless of the increase in popularity, the various empirical approaches should be thought of as strong complements, and combining insights from each of the methodologies will permit economists to develop a deeper understanding of our science.

References

Angner, Erik and Loewenstein, George. 2012. "Behavioral Economics" (January 14, 2007), in Uskali Maki (ed) *Handbook of the Philosophy of Science: Philosophy of Economics.* Amsterdam: Elsevier, pp. 641–690. Available at SSRN.

Branas-Garza, Pablo and Barreda, Ivan. 2015. "Experiments in Economics," in Branas-Garza, Pablo and Cabrales, Antonio (eds) *Experimental Economics, Volume 1: Economic Decisions.* New York: Palgrave Macmillan, pp. 1–16.

Chaudhuri, Ananish. 2009. *Experiments in Economics: Playing Fair with Money.* New York: Routledge.

Eckel, Catherine C. 2004. "Vernon Smith: Economics as a Laboratory Science," *Journal of Socio-Economics*, 33, 15–28.

Guala, Francesco. 2005. *The Methodology of Experimental Economics*. Cambridge: Cambridge University Press.

Guala, Francesco. 2010. "Experimental Economics, History of," in Durlauf, Steven N. and Blume, Lawrence E. (eds) *Behavioural and Experimental Economics*. New York: Palgrave Macmillan, pp. 99–106.

Heukelom, Floris. 2014. *Behavioral Economics: A History*. New York: Cambridge University Press.

List, John and Reiley, David. 2010. "Field Experiments," in Durlauf, Steven N. and Blume, Lawrence E. (eds) *Behavioural and Experimental Economics*. New York: Palgrave Macmillan, 151–156.

Smith, Vernon L. 1989. "Theory, Experiment and Economics," *Journal of Economic Perspectives*, 3(1), Winter, 151–169.

Smith, Vernon L. 1994. "Economics in the Laboratory," *Journal of Economic Perspectives*, 8(1), Winter, 113–131.

Smith, Vernon L. 2000. "Experimental Economics," in *International Encyclopedia of the Social and Behavioral Sciences*, 5100–5108.

Thaler, Richard H. 2015. *Misbehaving: The Making of Behavioral Economics*. New York: Norton.

11 Are mainstream economists open-minded toward behavioral economics or do they resist it?

The open-mindedness of mainstream economists

Confronted with new ideas, can we expect scholars to give them open-minded consideration? In an ideal world, scholars doing research would be completely open-minded when it comes to considering research findings that are dramatically at odds with the theories and perspectives they hold dear. That is, after a careful and thorough examination and thinking about the new research findings and with further time for reflection, open-minded scholars would adopt the new theories and perspectives and then let go of those to which they had previously been attached. Alas, the world is not ideal. This seems particularly true in the case of how most mainstream economists have responded to the challenge that behavioral economics (BE) has presented to their theories and values. Mainstream economists have greatly resisted the challenge presented by BE. Matthew Rabin and Richard Thaler in particular have written about this. According to Rabin (2002, p. 659), "the amount of time and intellectual energy – by journal editors, graduate advisors, and seminar audiences – devoted to articulating reasons why the [BE] research should not be done is still too high." And according to Thaler (2016, p. 1), "the behavioral approach to economics [has] met with considerable resistance within the profession." It is, of course, notable that both Rabin and Thaler have acknowledged that the resistance to BE has substantially declined in recent years. Let's further consider their thoughts and observations.

The resistance to BE by mainstream economists could be interpreted as in Kuhn as a phenomenon associated with the emergence of a new paradigm. As Kuhn (1970) has explained, the new rival paradigm will be strongly resisted by researchers who are steeped in and dedicated to the prevailing paradigm. It is noteworthy, however, that neither Thaler nor Rabin consider BE to be a new scientific paradigm. In Thaler's view, it is a misreading of the history of economic thought to consider the emergence of BE as a paradigm shift. According to Thaler (2016, p. 1), "it would be more accurate to say that the methodology of behavioral economics returns economic thinking to the way it began with Adam Smith and continued through to the time of Irving Fisher and John Maynard Keynes in the 1930s." Similarly, Rabin (2002, p.659) states that BE "is not an alternative to [NE] research but the natural continuation of this research program." Despite these views of Thaler and Rabin, the manner in which mainstream economists have responded to BE does seem to suggest that something like paradigm change has been involved with the rise of BE. Mainstream economists have often reacted to BE in a defensive, possibly threatened way. They typically have not reacted as if the BE being brought to their attention was merely just another fact or theory. It should, of course, be noted that now that BE has made progress, gained many adherents, demonstrated its importance, and gained significant recognition, many more economists are becoming open-minded toward it.

How mainstream economists react: defending the rationality assumption

One way that mainstream economists have reacted to BE is to defend the core assumptions of mainstream economics, particularly the assumption of rational behavior. Perhaps the best known and most effective defense of rationality is the one offered by Milton Friedman (1953). "He argued that theories should not be evaluated on the basis of the validity of their assumptions, but rather the accuracy of their predictions. An expert billiards player, he noted, may not know the laws of physics, but acts *as if* he knows such laws" (Thaler 1996, pp.227–228). The expert pool player using his eyes and good coordination acts as if he knew the complicated mathematical formulas of physics that would determine the optimum path that the ball should travel to reach the desired results. Thus, analogously, Friedman argues that competent business owners might not know how to calculate marginal costs and revenues in order to maximize profit but would nevertheless make decisions that closely approximate profit maximization using their superior intuitions (Thaler 2016, pp.3–4). Friedman's argument was successful in ending the debate about the realism of the rationality assumption. But there are problems in Friedman's *as if* argument. "First of all, it is no accident that Friedman chooses to discuss an expert billiards player. The behavior of an expert in many activities may indeed be well captured by a model that assumes optimal behavior. But what about non-experts?"

(p. 4). Economic theory is supposed to be a theory about the behavior of all economic actors, not just expert ones.

Another consideration related to the above defense of rational decision making is the degree of difficulty involved in a task. Economic agents may come close to maximizing their utility (or profit) in relatively easy tasks such as deciding how many eggs to buy for family breakfasts for the coming week. For tasks like buying eggs or milk, you can likely master the process by trial and error learning. After all, if you buy too much, it goes bad, and if you buy too little, it involves extra trips to the store (p. 6). People, however, are unlikely to do nearly as well (certainly not maximizing) in deciding on the right amount to save for retirement (p. 3). This is because there is no opportunity for using trial and error. This also applies to a great extent to buying a car or home, selecting a career, or choosing a spouse (p. 6). Unlike the oft repeated tasks, the latter are not done frequently, and they involve a great deal of uncertainty and difficulty. When there is a great amount of task difficulty, even experts will not be able to maximize (p. 4).

A second type of defense of the rationality assumption "is to concede that we don't all do everything like experts but argue that, if our errors are randomly distributed with mean zero, then they will wash out in the aggregate, leaving the predictions of the model unbiased on average" (Thaler 2016, p. 4). This argument has been refuted by the research of Kahneman and Tversky, who have argued that humans make judgments and decisions that are systematically and predictably biased, and thereby, are not rational even on the average. A third defense of the rationality assumption involves the idea that people, if not initially behaving rationally, will learn to choose more rationally. Unfortunately, there is much experimental evidence that is dubious about this idea. In general, psychologists find that "learning takes place when there is useful, immediate feedback . . . [and that] learning can be difficult even in a very simple environment" (p. 7).

A fourth argument why mainstream economics should retain the maximizing assumption is simply that irrationality is self-defeating. It is argued that if people choose in ways that are not fully rational they will ultimately lose out relative to people who are behaving fully rationally. This is either because of long-running evolutionary processes or because rational agents' market performance will be superior, leading them to attain higher income and wealth (Thaler 1996, pp. 228–229). The problem with this argument is, as Thaler points out, that the pressures of survival either in primitive societies or in modern markets are not very likely to lead to more or less survival depending on whether people adopt strict optimizing behavior.

How mainstream economists react: criticizing valid behavioral economic tenets

Behavioral economists have undeniably integrated many behavioral findings from psychology and elsewhere with economics, and this has led to greater understanding of how human behavior systematically departs from the core assumptions of mainstream economics. According to Rabin (2002, p. 658), the resulting departures are "fundamentally and manifestly good economics." Yet mainstream economists often react very negatively to these BE propositions when they (and the evidence for them) are brought to their attention. In essence, mainstream economists generally subscribe to NE and accordingly assume 100 percent self-interest, 100 percent rationality, and 100 percent self-control. Mainstream economics also makes many ancillary assumptions, typically used in specific models. Further, it is increasingly apparent that the core assumptions and many of the ancillary ones are not supported by economically relevant behavioral evidence (p. 658). When these findings have been brought to the attention of mainstream economists, Rabin has observed that the resistant verbal reactions of mainstream economists typically fall into a few characteristic patterns.

The first of the objections that Rabin has heard from economists who are resistant to greater psychological realism is: "We can't consider all alternatives." In other words, these "economists worry that if we allow new assumptions, then researchers could come along and assume anything" (Rabin 2002, p. 675). Economists have apparently feared that the broadening of economics by behavioral economists "will turn it into an undisciplined non-discipline, with no restrictions whatsoever on our assumptions" (p. 676). In Rabin's view, this mainstream complaint may have some merit but it is mostly misguided. He does acknowledge that sometimes the complexity of actual human behavior does require a wider range of assumptions, but this does not mean that behavioral economists would be apt to propose any kind of new assumptions at random (p. 676).

A second common objection of mainstream economists is: "That assumption was not in our graduate microeconomics text; therefore, it is some random assumption that you're making up" (Rabin 2002, p. 676). According to Rabin, although the assumption in question was likely not part of economic graduate students' education, it most likely was covered in a graduate psychology course and may have even been something that was learned before graduate school. Mainstream economists should not reject behavioral assumptions for the above reason. They should carefully examine the assumption to determine if it is behaviorally true or not, and use it only if it is true (p. 676).

A third objection of mainstream economists is: "Thomas Kuhn says we shouldn't 'think outside the box' . . . until the box is wholly shattered" (Rabin 2002, p. 677). In other words, this saying advocates not trying to make particular, small behavioral improvements in economics until the entire NE paradigm is proven wholly false and replaced. Such advice would be difficult to follow because it implies that we cannot make any progress until a scientific revolution has fully taken place. Rabin, on the other hand, advocates making behavioral changes, even very small ones, if they are behaviorally true.

A fourth objection of mainstream economists is a variant of the third one. It is: "If it ain't broke, don't fix it" (Rabin 2002, p. 677). It stems from the fear that efforts to improve economics might wind up making things worse. Why take such a chance if there is no obvious problem? According to Rabin, "It is illogical to doubt a behavioral hypothesis by showing that the standard hypothesis being challenged is not 100% wrong. The right question is whether standard [NE] assumptions are less than 100% right, and whether the shortfalls are sufficiently identifiable, sufficiently systematic, and sufficiently important that economists should study them" (p. 677).

The fifth and last mainstream objection is: "Markets will wipe (any unfamiliar psychological phenomenon) out" (Rabin 2002, p. 678). This means that economists should not introduce unfamiliar new behavioral assumptions, because these behaviors would not be expected to survive in markets. In Rabin's view, such "wipe-out arguments" are typically logically wrong and bad economics (p. 678). He believes it is not a good idea to ignore real psychological phenomena regardless of what is happening in markets.

Conclusion

Mainstream economists have until recently resisted new behavioral assumptions that depart from 100 percent self-interest, 100 percent rationality, and 100 percent self-control, and have done so based on economically flawed arguments (Rabin 2002, p. 685). Similarly, they have resisted modifications that would have improved the psychological realism of economics (p. 685). But as economists are coming to realize that greater psychological realism will improve, rather than undermine economics, such defensive arguments are decreasing. The upshot is that "economists are less and less employing bad economics to dismiss the relevance of good psychology, and more and more using good economics to absorb the lessons of the good psychology" (p. 685). It is Thaler's (2016, p. 19) hope that this growing acceptance of a behaviorally realistic economics signals that economists are turning their attention to the study of humans, not econs (economic men).

References

Friedman, Milton. 1953. "The Methodology of Positive Economics," in Friedman, Milton. *Essays on Positive Economics*. Chicago: University of Chicago Press, 3–34.

Kuhn, Thomas. 1970. *The Structure of Scientific Revolutions*, 2nd Edition. Chicago: University of Chicago Press.

Rabin, Matthew. 2002. "A Perspective on Psychology and Economics," *European Economic Review*, 46, 657–685.

Thaler, Richard H. 1996. "Doing Economics without *Homo Economicus*," in Medema, Steven G. and Samuels, Warren J. (eds) *Foundations of Research in Economics: How Do Economists Do Economics?* Cheltenham, UK and Brookfield, VT: Edward Elgar Publishing, pp. 227–337.

Thaler, Richard H. 2016. "Behavioral Economics: Past, Present, and Future," May 27. Available at SSRN: https://ssrn.com/abstract= 2790606.

12 Neuroeconomics

The essence of neuroeconomics

The discipline of neuroeconomics emerged around the year 2000. It integrates the theories of economics and psychology with neuroscience. This new field is noted for using neuroscience measurement technologies to understand how human brains function especially in the context of decision making. This is an important development because economists in their theorizing have treated the human brain as a "black box" (Coricelli and Nagel 2015, p. 135). Using neuroscience brain imaging technologies and other techniques, neuroeconomists have been able to gain important insights into how human brains function and how that relates to human economic behavior. According to Camerer (2008, p. 416):

> The long-run goal of neuroeconomics is to create a theory of economic choice and exchange that is neurally detailed, mathematically accurate, and behaviorally relevant. This theory will result from collaborations between neuroscientists and economists and will benefit from input from other fields, including computer science and psychology.

Neuroeconomic technologies

Neuroeconomics uses a variety of neuroscience measurement techniques to identify the neural underpinnings associated with economic decisions, and thereby to discover the proximate causes of human choice behavior (Zak 2004, p. 1737). Neuroscience methods include single-neuron recording, functional magnetic resonance imaging (fMRI), transcranial magnetic stimulation (TMS), lesion studies with brain-damaged patients, positron emission tomography (PET), electro-encephalogram (EEG) and event related potentials (ERP), and bioassays of blood, urine, or cerebral spinal fluid (p. 1739; Coricelli and Nagel 2015, p. 136). Both fMRI and PET imaging are based on measures of blood flow in different brain areas. Blood flow in these different areas reflects brain activity, in particular the rate of firing of neurons in that area. "When neurons fire, they deplete glucose and oxygen and require increased blood flow to resupply these substances. [Accordingly] blood flows to neurons roughly proportionally to their firing rates" (Zak 2004, p. 1739). When PET imaging is used, a computer measures the brain area's blood flow to provide an indirect measure of neural activity. Although fMRI technology works differently, it too produces signals related to blood flow that indirectly measure neural activity. When neural firing uses up oxygen and increases the demand for oxygenated blood, the fMRI process calculates and then utilizes a precise measure of the relative amounts of oxygenated to deoxygenated blood using a very powerful magnet. Based on this, an fMRI computer algorithm constructs a three-dimensional image of neural activity (p. 1739). The fMRI and PET imaging technologies are used in most neuroeconomic research performed on humans (p. 1739). fMRI is particularly important; its use to obtain images of human cognitive processes has grown exponentially. This rapid growth is explained by the fact that fMRI is widely available, safe, and provides visually compelling images that show activated brain areas "lighting up" (Glimcher and Fehr 2013, p. xxii).

Essential elements of brain functioning

Based on the above, one could easily come to the conclusion that the purpose of the brain research that uses imaging technologies is to learn "where things happen in the brain" and how human behaviors are associated with brain region activity (Camerer, Loewenstein, and Prelec 2004, p. 8). However, it should be noted that the long-run goal of neuroeconomics is not just to map the brain. The goal is also to understand how the interaction of different parts of the brain enables humans to solve different types of problems and make different kinds of decisions (p. 8). To fully understand brain (or neural) functioning, it is necessary to make two kinds of distinctions. The first distinction is between automatic and controlled processing (p. 10). In Chapter 4 of this book, these two types of processing were referred to as the Automatic System (or System 1) and the Reflective System (or System 2) decision making processes. On the one hand, automatic processes are relatively effortless, rapid, intuitive, spontaneous, and not accessible to consciousness (p. 11). On the other hand, controlled processes are the opposite; they are relatively slow, effortful, logical, and deliberate. "Automatic and controlled processes can be roughly distinguished by where they occur in the brain" (p. 11). Controlled processes are located in the front (or prefrontal) parts of the cortex (the higher areas of the brain). The prefrontal cortex is known as the "executive region, because it draws inputs from almost all other regions, integrates them to form near and long-term goals, and plans actions that takes these goals into account" (p. 12). The automatic brain processes tend to be located in the middle brain region below the cortex. This area is known as the limbic system. One of its important structures is the amygdala which is responsible for many important automatic brain responses.

The second important brain functioning distinction is that between the brain's cognitive processes and its affective (or emotional) processes. On the one hand, the brain's cognitive processes relate to thinking, learning, and understanding activities. Cognitive processes are associated with efforts to understand the truth or falsity of statements about the world. On the other hand, affective processes are associated with our feelings. Humans have positive and negative feelings and experience more or less intense emotions (Camerer, Loewenstein, and Prelec 2004, p. 13). It is our emotions that motivate us to act. For example, anger can motivate us to be aggressive, and fear might motivate us to escape or freeze (p. 13). Note that the term, affect, also includes "drive states such as hunger, thirst, and sexual desire as well as other motivational states such as physical pain, discomfort (e.g., nausea) and drug craving" (p. 13).

The first two types of brain processing, automatic and controlled, along with the other two types, cognitive and affective, define four quadrants, which correspond to four types of brain behavior. Quadrant 1 includes brain processing that is controlled and cognitive. Quadrant 4 includes brain processing that is automatic and affective. Much brain behavior lies in Quadrants 1 and 4; it is either controlled and cognitive or automatic and affective. Quadrant 2, controlled and affective, is rare, and Quadrant 3, automatic and cognitive, is less common and less significant than Quadrants 1 and 4. So for practical and economic modeling purposes, it is fair to say that "cognition is typically controlled, and affect is automatic." That is, there are essentially two types of brain processing, not four (Camerer, Loewenstein, and Prelec 2004, p. 14).[1]

Another way to understand brain processing is through the use of a two-system approach, one hot and the other cool (Metcalfe and Mischel 1999). The hot and cool systems approach overlaps with the four Quadrant approach in the sense that the cool state is akin to cognitive/controlled brain processing and the hot state is akin to emotional/automatic brain processing. The essence of hot and cool systems was explained in Chapter 5 in the context of how a person's emotions influence his/her decision making. The hot system is associated with the following characteristics: emotional, simple, fast, and accentuated by stress. The characteristics associated with the cool system are: cognitive, complex, slow, attenuated by stress, and self-control (p. 4). Hot and cool systems are essentially about self-control and self-regulation. More specifically, they are about the "ability [of a person] to inhibit an impulsive response that undoes one's commitment," thereby thwarting one's best intentions (p. 3). When our hot and cool systems are working in a well-balanced way, we have the ability to restrain our responses to temptations and delay our gratifications. Ideally, the hot and cool systems enable a person to regulate themselves over extended periods of time. In doing this, these systems demand strategic mobilization of thought, feeling, and coordinated action, enabling a person to act in a coordinated way and to take control of potentially problematic situations (p. 4). In Chapter 5, male college students' sexual arousal was used as an example of a hot state, which was found to strongly influence their attitudes and decision making propensities. In the throes of such a hot state, these young men seemed to lose their ability for self-control. But in their more typical cool states, these young men acted reasonably and were self-controlled.

To fully appreciate the importance of the two-system approach, it is important to consider it in the context of human development. As humans become more mature, developing along various pathways, the relative importance of their hot and cool systems changes. "The hot system develops early, whereas the cool system develops later. Thus during the earliest years of life the hot system is functioning, whereas the cool system remains largely undeveloped" (Metcalfe and Mischel 1999, p. 8). A young child asked to make a choice between a cookie now or two cookies tomorrow typically has little capacity to wait until tomorrow, i.e., the child has little capacity to delay gratification. This indicates that in contrast to their hot system, their cool system is not well developed. However, as the child ages, his/her cool system develops, and there is a "shift of dominance from the hot to the cool system" (p. 8). This understanding of development is consistent with evidence that the amygdala (part of the brain's hot system) "is functioning at birth, whereas the hippocampus and frontal lobe structures [associated with the brain's cool system] . . . become fully mature only sometime well after birth" (p. 8). The changing dominance of hot and cold systems is also consistent with the view that certain higher aspects of development such as elements of emotional intelligence take a long time to develop and may never be developed by some (p. 16).

Another important factor that affects the operation of the hot and cool systems is stress. The impact of stress on each of the two systems is very different. With the hot system, greater stress increases its effect up to very high levels. However, with the cool system, increases in stress at first improve its performance as arousal occurs. "However, as the stress level increases, the cool system becomes increasingly dysfunctional, leaving the hot system to dominate processing" (Metcalfe and Mischel 1999, p. 8). This makes sense from the standpoint of human mental performance. "At low levels of stress, it is to the organism's advantage to take in as much information as possible and to store it in a neutral manner for later remembrances and uses. This allows for complex thinking, planning, and remembering" (p. 8). However, at high levels of stress, especially when a human's life may be threatened, very quick responses to trigger stimuli are of utmost importance, not careful, slow, complex thinking and planning (p. 8).

An important piece of history

To get some historical perspective on neuroeconomics, let's consider a particularly interesting event that occurred in 1848 in the state of Vermont (U.S.). It concerns the case of Phineas Gage, a 25-year-old construction foreman who was in charge of a group of men who were building a railroad across Vermont (Damasio 1994, pp. 3–19). To do this, it was sometimes necessary to use explosives to blast away stone in the railroad's path. One afternoon, a bad accident occurred; instead of blasting away the stone, the blast blew up prematurely in Gage's face. It caused an iron bar to pierce his skull and to traverse the front of his brain and then to exit at high speed out through the top of his head. Surprisingly, Gage recovered physically from the accident in only two months, but it soon became clear that mentally he had dramatically changed for the worse. Up to that time, Gage had been acknowledged to be "the most efficient and capable man" employed by his company (p. 4). Gage's doctor recounted that "the equilibrium or balance, so to speak, between his intellectual faculty and animal propensities had been destroyed" (p. 8). His mental change was radical; the people who knew him said that "Gage was no longer Gage" (p. 8). Gage had lost "something in the brain [that] was concerned specifically with unique human properties, among them the ability to anticipate the future and plan accordingly, ... the sense of responsibility toward the self and others, and the ability to orchestrate one's survival deliberately" (p. 10). "After the accident, he no longer showed respect for social conventions," and he generally behaved unethically (p. 11). Despite his degenerated character, Gage's attention, perception, memory, language, and intelligence were intact.

Making sense of the unfortunate accident

What can students of the brain learn from what happened to Gage's brain? At the time of Gage's accident, there were very few specialists in brain science. And, among them, some believed that brain functions could not be traced to particular brain regions. Others believed that "the brain did have specialized parts and those parts generated separate mind functions" (Damasio 1994, p. 12). One of the latter was the British physiologist David Ferrier who competently analysed the Gage findings. "He concluded that the wound spared motor and language 'centers,' that it did damage ... the prefrontal cortex, and that such damage might be related to Gage's peculiar change in personality" (p. 14). That was the best that brain science could do for very many years. Beginning in the 1990s, "systematic study of decision-making deficits following brain damage was undertaken ... by Antonio Damasio, Antoine Bechara and their colleagues" (Glimcher and Fehr 2014, p. xxii). These researchers, using Gage's preserved skull, were able to confirm that the iron bar passing through Gage's brain "did not touch the brain regions necessary for motor function or language" (p. 32). They also concluded that other brain regions would have been intact. Thus, in the view of these researchers, Gage's compromised abilities were only due to the damage to his prefrontal cortex.

Besides the Gage incident and related brain research, scientists now understand that there are many kinds of brain damage (chronic mental illnesses (e.g., schizophrenia), developmental disorders (e.g., autism), degenerative diseases of the nervous system, and accidents and strokes) that can damage localized brain regions (Camerer, Loewenstein, and Prelec 2004, p. 7). How can these various types of brain damage help us gain definitive understanding of brain functioning? "When patients with known damage to ... [brain] area X perform a special task more poorly than 'normal' patients, and do other tasks equally well, one can infer that area X is used to do the special task" (p. 7). Based on the historical evidence and logical reasoning, it is now quite clear that Gage's severely impaired social and individual decision making was caused by the accident that damaged his prefrontal cortex. The research of Damasio and colleagues has persuasively explained how Gage's and other similar brain damaged persons' poor behavior is not due to lack of knowledge or intelligence. The impaired decision making is because Gage and others with similar damage are unable to integrate their emotional experience with their cognitive functioning.[2]

Toward improved understanding of brain functioning

The research on brain injuries such as that mentioned above were no doubt very important in providing fundamental early insight into the human brain's functioning. However, to gain greater understanding of many aspects of brain functioning, especially economic decision making, requires the "development of methods to image human brain activity non-invasively" (Glimcher and Fehr 2014, p. xxii). The use of fMRI imaging technology mentioned earlier is a prime example. It has become possible to obtain direct images of human brain activity while subjects are engaged in cognitive tasks. The experiments that use brain imaging typically "involve a comparison of people performing different tasks – an 'experimental' task and a 'control' task. The difference between images taken while a subject is performing the two tasks" enables the researchers to obtain a "picture of regions of the brain that are differentially activated by the experimental task" (Camerer, Loewenstein, and Prelec 2004, p. 4). And these images enable the researchers to make inferences about the role that the different parts of the brain are playing, with regard to the different types of cognitive activity.

Examples of neuroeconomic research

An interesting and important early example of neuroeconomic research appears in an article entitled "The Neural Basis of Economic Decision-Making in the Ultimatum Game" (Sanfey et al. 2003). (Recall that the Ultimatum Game (UG) was described in detail in Chapter 5.) The authors analysed the decisions of people playing the UG. After the initial analysis, researchers used fMRI brain imaging to interpret how subjects made their choices. As you may recall, in the UG, a proposer is given a sum of money to divide between his/her self and the responder. The proposer could be generous and fair, and accordingly divide the sum 50–50, or she could divide the sum in an unequal and unfair way, for example 80–20. In the case of an unequal and unfair division of the sum, the responder may decide to reject the proposer's offer. In that case, neither the proposer nor responder would receive anything.

What can we learn about brain functioning by using fMRI imaging to examine the decision making of the responder? Consider the decisions and motivation of the responder. On the one hand, the responder wants as much money as possible and thus wants to make a smart choice with this in mind. On the other hand, the responder presumably wants to be treated fairly; he or she does not want to be taken advantage of. There is, thus, a mix of motivations: both economic rationality and a kind of social motivation. The findings from many UG experiments indicate that responders are often very unhappy with low, unfair offers and reject them. Responders' rejection of such offers does not make sense from the standpoint of strict economic rationality. This is because such responders are choosing a lower payoff. Perhaps in such cases, the responders are angry with the proposer. Apparently, the responders not only care about fairness but also want to retaliate against people they regard as unfair jerks, and they want to make sure that these people are punished.

In their use of fMRI imaging, Sanfey and his colleagues focused on the brain activity of responders who received unfair offers. The responders typically experienced a conflict between their cognitive (accept) motive and their emotional (reject) motive. The responders in the experiment accepted all fair offers but the more unfair the offers were, the more they were rejected. The authors "hypothesized that unfair offers would engage neural structures involved in both emotional and cognitive processing, and that the magnitude of activation in these structures might explain variance in the subsequent decision to accept or reject these offers" (Sanfey et al. 2003, p. 1756). The results of the experiment for rejected offers were that responders' brains had a high degree of activation of the anterior insula, the prefrontal cortex (dorsolateral part), and the anterior cingulate cortex. "Anterior insula activation is consistently seen in neuroimaging studies of pain and distress and hunger and thirst . . . . This region has also been implicated in studies of emotion; in particular . . . negative emotional states . . . [notably] anger and disgust" (p. 1756). Further, subjects "with stronger anterior insula activation to unfair offers rejected a higher proportion of these offers" (p. 1757). The activation of the prefrontal cortex apparently relates to the cognitive demands of the task, namely thinking about how to achieve the goal of accumulating as much money as possible. The experimental evidence is thus consistent with the hypothesis. The UG responders are not behaving simply as profit or money maximizers; their emotions, particularly those related to fairness are strong and influential. Thus, emotions deriving from different regions in the limbic system as well as the prefrontal cortex have a very important and understandable role in human decision making.

Another important example of neuroeconomic research was published in *Neuron* in 2007 by Brian Knutson and his coauthors. The article is entitled "Neural Predictors of Purchases;" it investigates the key factors people consider when they make purchasing decisions (Knutson et al. 2007). According to mainstream microeconomic theory, a person's decision to purchase a good is based on his/her preference for the good (given its characteristics) and its price. Essentially, the theory is that people buy products that they are attracted to and attempt to avoid paying excessively high prices for them (p. 147). Behavioral versions of this purchase theory emphasize that people seek immediate pleasure (a gain) from their acquisitions of goods and seek to avoid the immediate pain of paying (a loss) (p. 147). Not surprisingly, people are hypothesized to buy goods for which the gains outweigh the losses. In order to test this theory using brain imaging technology (notably fMRI), it is necessary to make some revisions to the theory. In the revised version, a person is expected to buy a good when the individual's net anticipated affect from buying the good is favorable. The anticipated affect is determined from neuroimaging evidence of activity in different neural circuits. There is increasing "neuroimaging evidence suggesting that activity in different neural circuits correlates with positive and negative anticipatory affect" (p. 147). The anticipation of gains from purchases has been found to activate the nucleus accumbens, and that activation correlates with self-reported positive arousal, and thus gain prediction. On the other hand, anticipation of physical pain activates the insula, and that correlates with self-reported negative arousal. "The insula has been hypothesized to play a critical role in loss prediction" (p. 147). Therefore, the evidence indicates that activation in both the nucleus accumbens and the insula circuits influence subsequent choice.

The goal of the Knutson study was to determine whether anticipatory activation obtained from several brain regions could independently predict subjects' subsequent decisions to purchase particular goods

(Knutson et al. 2007, p. 148). Based on the fMRI imaging results, the researchers were able to predict that when subjects considered certain goods, they would choose to buy goods that activated circuits associated with anticipated gain. Similarly, researchers predicted that when subjects considered prices, excessive prices would activate their brain circuits associated with anticipated loss (p. 148). Further, the experimental results were able to predict whether individuals would subsequently choose to purchase a product. According to the authors:

> we hypothesized and found that activation in regions associated with anticipating gain (the nucleus accumbens) correlated with product preference, while activation in regions associated with anticipating loss (the insula) correlated with excessive prices . . . . Together, these findings suggest that activation of distinct brain regions related to anticipation of gain and loss precedes and can be used to predict purchasing decisions (p. 152)

> The findings support the historical notion that individuals have immediate affective reactions to potential gain and loss, which serve as inputs into decisions about whether or not to purchase a product. (p. 153)

Putting neuroeconomics in perspective

It is important to point to a number of limitations of studies that use neuroimaging methods like the ones discussed above. First, "the signal that we measure with fMRI is just a proxy for brain activity; . . . it is only an approximation of actual brain activity" (Coricelli and Nagel 2015, p. 151). This means that we have to be careful not to be overly confident in discovering relationships when we interpret neuroeconomic findings. Second, when interpreting "neuroimaging data, it is important not to jump to the conclusion that there is a causal relationship involved" (p. 151). It may be incorrect to say that a certain brain area A causes function X. It may only be correct to talk about the correlation between a brain area's activation and subsequent behavioral functioning. Other interpretive difficulties can be involved because many brain areas function in a variety of different ways (p. 151). The upshot is that neuroimaging technologies can serve as powerful, non-invasive tools for learning about brain processes, but they need to be used and interpreted with considerable care.

Neuroeconomics is important because it "provides a unified framework to measure neurophysiological activity during the process of choice, and in doing so opens a window into human nature" (Zak 2004, p. 1746).

> The challenge of neuroeconomics is to develop more ... valid models of economic behavior, integrating the influence of social, cultural and emotional influences on economic decision making .... The expected benefits are: 1) a better understanding of the cerebral, cognitive, and cultural underpinnings of social cognition; 2) eventually the possibility of helping patients with behavioral deficits toward a better social life; [and] 3) a greater degree of insight into precisely what it means to be rational. (Coricelli and Nagel 2015, p. 153)

NOTES

1 It should be noted that a substantial amount of cognitive processing is automatic, e.g., language processing.

2 As brain scientists have discovered, there is a part of the prefrontal cortex that is at the interface of emotion and cognition. When this part is damaged, the kind of mental difficulty that Gage had is experienced (Coricelli and Nagel 2015, p. 141).

References

Camerer, Colin F. 2008. "Neuroeconomics: Opening the Gray Box," *Neuron*, 60(3), November 6, 416–419.

Camerer, Colin F., Loewenstein, George and Prelec, Drazen. 2004. "Neuroeconomics: How Neuroscience Can Inform Economics," *Journal of Economic Literature*, forthcoming. Available at SSRN (https://ssrn.com/abstract=590965).

Coricelli, Giorgio and Nagel, Rosemarie. 2015. "Responses from the Body: An Introduction to Neuroeconomics," in Branas-Garza, Pablo and Cabrales, Antonio (eds) *Experimental Economics, volume 1 Economic Decisions*. New York: Palgrave Macmillan, 135–153.

Damasio, Antonio R. 1994. *Descartes' Error: Emotion, Reason, and the Human Brain*. New York: Avon Books.

Glimcher, Paul W. and Fehr, Ernst. 2013. "Introduction: A Brief History of Neuroeconomics," in Glimcher, Paul W. and Fehr, Ernst (eds) *Neuroeconomics: Decision Making and the Brain*. 2nd Edition. Cambridge, MA: Academic Press, xvi–xxviii.

Knutson, Brian et al. 2007. "Neural Predictors of Purchases," *Neuron*, 53(1), 147–156.

Metcalfe, Janet and Mischel, Walter. 1999. "A Hot/Cool-System Analysis of Delay of Gratification: Dynamics of Willpower," *Psychological Review*, 106(1), 3–19.

Sanfey, Alan G. et al. 2003. "The Neural Basis of Economic Decision-Making in the Ultimatum Game," *Science*, 300(5626), June 13, 1755–1758.

Zak, Paul J. 2004. "Neuroeconomics," *Philosophical Transactions of the Royal Society B*, 359, November, 1737–1748.

13 Toward a more humanistic behavioral economics

A humanistic behavioral economics

Arguably, economics needs a more humanistic orientation. What do we mean by humanism? Humanism is a system of thought that focuses on humans, particularly their behavior, values, capacities, and worth. It emphasizes reason and moral values founded on human nature. Also, humanism reflects the human values of ancient Greece and Rome. Is behavioral economics (BE) as I have described it in the earlier chapters of this book humanistic? Yes, it has elements of humanism. BE is certainly more humanistic than neoclassical economics (NE). For example, Herbert Simon's writings on human decision making, and bounded rationality more generally, are certainly much more humanistic than NE's depictions of decision making and rationality. However, I believe that a more humanistic BE would be an important improvement. In recent years, a number of BE scholars have written thoughtful contributions that I consider to be important elements of a more humanistic BE. This chapter summarizes three of these important contributions. These are relatively recent writings that are not widely recognized. As a result, this chapter differs from the main thrust of the book's other chapters that on the whole have presented widely recognized BE concepts. It is noteworthy that the authors of the writings summarized in this chapter are scholars who have made significant BE contributions. The first of the writings summarized below has been referred to as dual motive theory. The second derives from Akerlof and Shiller's book, *Phishing for Phools.* The third comes from Paul Zak's work that deals with the human molecule known as oxytocin and its relation to the economy.

Dual motive theory: the core underlying human motivations

The essence of dual motive theory

The two core human motivations are self-interest and other interest. The starting point for understanding these two motivations is Paul MacLean's (1990) research on brain physiology. He conceived of the human brain as having three interconnected modular levels. The first part of the brain, the earliest in evolutionary terms, is the innermost core of the brain, the reptilian complex, which governs fundamental physiological operations and is concerned with self-preservation (Tomer 2012, p. 78). It is associated with self-interest motivation. The second brain module, the paleomammalian brain, is located on top of the reptilian brain. It provides for the distinctively mammalian features of humans such as maternal care, parental responsibility, family life, and social bonding. This part of the brain is associated with caring, other interest, and empathic motivation. The third brain is the neo-mammalian brain or neocortex that envelops the other two brains. This brain provides the human capacities for problem solving, learning, memory, language, thinking, and related functions. According to MacLean, the neocortex is involved in determining how the two strong core motivations, empathy deriving from the paleomammalian brain and self-interest deriving from the reptilian brain, are interrelated and expressed. This dual human motivation view deriving from MacLean's research is in sharp contrast to mainstream economics' view of humans as motivated solely by self-interest.[1]

Based on the brain physiology research of MacLean, Gerald Cory (1999) developed a model explaining how the two core human motivations tend to be balanced. In his view, it is the executive functioning of the brain's neocortex that attempts to bring about a balance between the self-interest and empathy motivations that frequently are in conflict with each other (Tomer 2012, pp. 78–9). Cory's brain model involves a homeostatic process that tends to reduce the tension and stress associated with imbalance and tends to bring about a favorable balance between the two motivations, a balance associated with reciprocity, cooperation, fairness, and morality.

The dual motive theory (DMT) of MacLean/Cory has important implications for the model of the human brain's functioning used in economics. Obviously, it implies that people have two dominant motivations, ego or self-interest and empathy or other-interest.[2] Further, it implies that the meaning of rationality in DMT is different from its meaning in the mainstream economic model (Tomer 2012, p. 80). Rationality in the DMT model does not involve simply maximizing the self's utility. Rationality as in DMT involves attempting to do well for oneself as well as attempting to do well by others. In the DMTs broad conception of rationality, the essence of rational behavior is attempting to live a well-balanced life in which one's own interests are integrated with others.

Tomer (2012) has proposed a revised DMT model that incorporates recent insights from brain science. In the revised model, an individual's empathic capacity is determined not just by genetics but also by brain changes that happen as a consequence of the individual's life experience. The latter phenomenon is known as brain plasticity; it is the ability of the brain to change structurally and functionally as a result of input from the environment (p. 81). Although every human has basically the same brain physiology, a particular person's brain functioning is also shaped by that individual's unique path through life. That is, an individual's capacities such as his/her empathic capacity are shaped by every sustained activity of the person, that is, all the person's physical activities, sensory activities, cultural activities, learning, thinking, imagining, etc. (Doidge 2007, pp. 287–91). In the revised DMT model of the human brain's functioning, people still have two dominant motivations (ego and empathy), but the strength and character of an individual's empathic motivation depends very much on the individual's life experience and whether the individual has made efforts to develop his/her empathic capacity.

According to Lynne et al. (2015), the true relationship between the self-interest and empathy motivations is somewhat different from the relationship the DMT model articulates. According to Lynne et al., while the two motivations could be directly in conflict, generally the self-interest motive is primal, and a person's empathic capacity plays a restraining or conditioning role with respect to self-interest. This is particularly so when human self-interest is excessive. Excessive self-interest may manifest as egoistic, selfish, hedonistic, or greedy behavior. When this excess is present, humans are arguably in need of greater self-control. That is, it would be desirable if they would temper, restrain, or condition their self-interest motivation. Otherwise, the economy will not be sustainable because the economy will be dominated by the actions of individuals who do not consider the harm they impose on the public as a whole ("tragedy of the commons" situations) (Lynne et al. 2015). In a "good capital-ism," humans' empathy along with other human virtues play a very positive role, ideally leading humans to more balanced behavior that involves an integration of one's self-interest with the interests of others (McCloskey 2006). Interestingly as Lynne et al. (2015, pp. 1–3) notes, taken together Adam Smith's two books, *Wealth of Nations* (1776) and *The Theory of Moral Sentiments* (1759/1790), articulate the essence of this view.

Socio-economic dysfunction, social problems, and the underlying dual motivations

How, you might ask, is the above analysis of the underlying human factors, self-interest and empathy, related to the socio-economic dysfunction associated with social problems? Let's consider the prob-lem of obesity (see Tomer 2016, Chapters 6 and 8). At the heart of this problem is excessive, uninformed self-interest. First, too many food businesses have behaved in an opportunistic, unscrupulous, and greedy manner. These are businesses that are more than willing to take unfair advantage of their customers by selling them unhealthy foods, and that are unwilling to inquire into whether their practices are harmful to the consumers of their products. Second, many food consumers have also behaved opportunistically and ignorantly in the sense that they have sought to take advantage of foods that are appealing and low cost but which are unhealthy and harmful in the long run. Unfortunately, nei-ther of these excessively self-interested behaviors have been tempered, restrained, or conditioned to any extent by empathy and other virtues. Further, positive community and societal norms have apparently been too weak to restrain the forces of excessive business self-interest. And too many food consumers have been too preoccupied with their own self-interests to counter the unscrupulous food business behavior. If it were not for these underlying human factors, it seems very likely that early food experiences with increasing obesity and rising health prob-lems might have been recognized and reversed. But because excessive unrestrained self-interest, involving a lack of empathy and other vir-tues, are at the heart of the problem, the obesity problem has contin-ued with great force despite increasing knowledge of its patterns and the health science related to it.

There seem to be quite a few other situations where the underlying core human factors are the key culprit in the socio-economic dys-function at the heart of social problems. Certainly this is true for the chronic ailments that have causes very similar to those for obesity. But let's examine an example outside the health field, an example associated with the financial crisis of 2008, that is, the example of excessive mortgage lending. It is no secret that unscrupulous lenders made far too many subprime mortgage loans, especially to people who had little or no ability to repay these loans. These lenders then quickly sold these loans to securitizers (Blinder 2013, pp. 68–72). One example of this lending was the $720,000 mortgage loan to a pair of Mexican American strawberry pickers whose annual incomes were around $14,000. The loan enabled them to buy a $720,000 house (p. 69). During this time, many mortgage lenders were making "low-doc" mortgage loans with little documentation, "no-doc" mortgages with no documentation, "liar loans" with false documentation, and even some "NINJA" loans to people with no income, no jobs, and no assets (p. 70). These mortgage lenders were "making loans 'designed to default' to financially unsophisticated borrowers who likely did not know what they were getting themselves into . . . . [This] violates every principle of sound banking – not to mention human decency" (p. 71). Clearly, with respect to the lenders, these were examples of excessive self-interest run amok. It also does not reflect well on the recipients of these loans. It seems fairly obvious that this kind of situation could have been largely avoided if the lenders' self-interests had been tempered, restrained, and conditioned by other regarding motivations, not to mention governmental and societal norms and regulation.

Developing empathy and restraining excessive self-interest

Recall that MacLean's research on brain physiology makes it clear that both self-interest and empathy are inherent human motivations deriving from two different brain modules (and two different stages in brain evolution). But as more recent brain research has discovered, brain functioning is changeable or plastic. It follows that empathic capacity as well as how empathic capacity interacts with self-interest are subject to change for better or worse. What needs changing is the human tendency to be very selfish, opportunistic, unscrupulous, and greedy, the underlying cause of more than a few social problems. Fortunately, it is possible for humans to develop their dual motivations in a much more balanced and integrated way, achieving a more desirable mix of these two core motivations, a mix with much more empathy and a mix in which self-interest is restrained by other regarding interest. Therefore, it makes a lot of sense for a society to make the kinds of investment in human capitalism (HC) that lessen humans' excessive self-interest, thereby reducing socio-economic dysfunctions and remedying the corresponding social problems.

The payoff to improving the dual motivation

Actually measuring a society's payoff to improving humans' dual motivation via HC investments would be extremely difficult and is beyond the scope of this research. However, one can get some idea about the nature and rough magnitude of the payoff using reason and social science knowledge. So let's try a thought experiment. Suppose for the moment that societies could learn how to be highly successful in making the kind of investments in the underlying human factors suggested above. The question is: what is the likely payoff to a society from making these investments that would drastically lower socio-economic dysfunctions and dramatically reduce social problems. First, from the analyses in the sections above, we can confidently conclude that investments that are designed to improve a society's dual motivation would prevent financial crises and most obesity, and would largely prevent most chronic diseases. This means, among other things, greater health for citizens, lower costs of health care, and less need for health insurance. Further, if these investments resulted in a relative absence of severe opportunistic and unscrupulous behavior, another payoff would be the elimination of a great deal of financial and economic regulation. With a lot fewer resources being used for regulation and health care, many more resources would be available for other desired purposes. Arguably, as a result of such investments, people would be happier because they would be less selfish, that is, less focused on the things they want, and more focused on serving others. It might very well create a more moral, less stressful environment in the workplace, enabling greater worker satisfaction. As a result, people would be more self-controlled and more self-directed, and consequently, less tolerant of traditional forms of external, hierarchical control. Arguably, such a society would be more creative both at home and at work. Of course, it should be mentioned that the investment necessary to improve the underlying human factors would use up some resources that would have to be considered in tallying the investment's net payoff. Alas, this was only a thought experiment, but arguably a beneficial one. I believe it is useful because it is important to consider the full array of benefits that might result from making successful investments in improving the underlying human factors. This is so even if achieving such success would be very difficult to achieve. Note also that the impact of such successful HC investments could entail a dramatic move away from the traditional functioning of capitalism. The traditional capitalist system is generally thought to be a highly productive system in which moral standards in many respects are low. Successful investment in the underlying human factors would arguably create a capitalism that is not only highly productive but also highly moral.

Manipulation and deception in competitive markets

Why don't free competitive markets serve us well? In their book, *Phishing for Phools: The Economics of Manipulation and Deception*, George Akerlof and Robert Shiller (2015) develop a theory that explains why competitive markets are often dysfunctional in the sense of not serving the interests of market participants. In their explanations, they have used two words (phish and phool) associated with the Internet. People who phish are trying to get other people, the target people, to do things that are in the interests of the phishers or phishermen, but not in the interest of the target people. A phool is a target person who is successfully phished. According to the authors, there are two kinds of phools: psychological and informational (Akerlof and Shiller 2015, p. xi). Further, there are two types of psychological phools. In the first type, "the emotions of a psychological phool override the dictates of his common sense. In the other type, cognitive biases, which are like optical illusions, lead the phool to misinterpret reality, and he acts on the basis of that misinterpretation" (p. xi). Note that cognitive biases include the biases explained in Chapter 4 of this book. Among these biases are availability, anchoring, representativeness, status quo, endowment effect, and loss aversion. Lastly, information phools are people who "act on information that is intentionally crafted to mislead them" (p. xi).

There are two problematic aspects of competitive markets, that is, two market features that contribute to them becoming dysfunctional. The first relates to the incentives faced by would-be phishers. According to Akerlof and Shiller, the basic problem with those who phish is not a lack of morality or excessive self-interest. The essential problem derives from the pressures they experience for less than scrupulous behavior due to the incentives of competitive markets (p. xi). As Akerlof and Shiller see it, even relatively honest business managers are likely to be led by competitive pressures to phish in order to compete and survive (p. xii). On the other hand, business leaders who admirably exercise self-restraint, and do not take advantage of customers, are considered by the authors to be heroes.

The second problematic aspect of competitive markets relates to the phoolish nature of the people who are the targets of phishers. In the scenario depicted by Akerlof and Shiller, the key to these competitive market difficulties is that "people [who are the targets of the phishers] frequently make decisions that are not in their [own] best interest. Put bluntly, they do not do what is really good for themselves; they do not choose what they really want. Such bad decisions make it possible for them to be phished for phools" (Akerlof and Shiller 2015, p. 1). These bad decisions are a consequence of the psychological and informational factors mentioned above. When, because of people's bad decisions, there is an opportunity for above equilibrium (or above normal) profits to be made by phishing, some would-be phishers will act to take advantage of the opportunity, and thereby many of the target people are likely to have phoolishly taken the bait of the phishermen. This process has a tendency to continue until a new equilibrium is reached in which no more above normal profit phishing opportunities exist.

To get an idea of how dysfunctional markets might become, Akerlof and Shiller use the example of Capuchin monkeys. Research has shown that these monkeys can learn how to use money and acquire goods in markets (Akerlof and Shiller 2015, p. 4). They can appreciate prices and anticipate payoffs. Imagine an experiment in which these monkeys were given incomes and encouraged to buy goods in markets without any regulatory safeguards. Note that "Capuchins have limited ability to resist temptation" (p. 4). These monkeys will be able to get whatever they choose in the market. How would these monkeys behave? Obviously, they will buy whatever they want. The problem is that those choices are likely to be very different from what makes them happy. We know, for example, that Capuchins love Marshmallow Fluff-filled Fruit Roll-Ups (p. 4). It is unlikely that they would resist the Roll-Ups. Moreover, there is good reason to believe that as a result of their many bad choices, "they would become anxious, malnourished, exhausted, addicted, quarrelsome, and sickened" (p. 4). In other words, their free market choices would not be ones that make them better off.

This brings us to the example of Cinnabon, a company that makes a very tasty cinnamon roll that has an attractive smell, has 880 calories, and is slathered in frosting. It is very tempting to buy Cinnabons, but they are not a healthy food. The success of Cinnabon is an example of a company that has phished and found many phools to buy its product. It is an example of how "the free market system exploits our weaknesses" (pp. 2–3). There are many other such companies phishing in the same waters. One suspects that if Cinnabon had not introduced its cinnamon roll, some other company surely would have (p. 3). There is good reason to believe that customers' phoolish choices of Cinnabons are not in their best interests. Of course, buying a Cinnabon roll is not the worst mistake you can make in your life. To get a better idea of the full cost of phishing for phools, Akerlof and Shiller provide many other examples where the stakes are much higher. These examples include rip-offs in cars, houses, credit cards, politics, food, pharmaceuticals, innovative products, tobacco, alcohol, and finance. There is no doubt that humans are smarter and more capable of making good choices than Capuchin monkeys. But as Akerlof and Shiller (2015, p. 4) explain, humans in many contexts often make choices that are not much better than the Capuchins.

Contrasting the dual motive view with the phishing/ phool view

Akerlof and Shiller's analysis of the reasons why market economies are often dysfunctional differs in important ways from the analysis of dual motive theory that focuses on the two core human motivations. In the dual motive view, the general conclusion is that socio-economic dysfunction often occurs when the motivations of decision makers are excessively self-interested and characterized by too little empathy and regard for others. This perspective generally leads us to the conclusion that economic decision makers are to blame for the outcomes that are not good for us. In contrast, the phishing/phool analysis focuses on economic decision makers in competitive markets and how strong market competition can lead businesses to take advantage of their customers. In this view, it is customers who are more to blame because they have a strong tendency to make bad decisions for reasons related to their emotions, their cognitive biases, or their possession of misleading or false information.

On reflection, these two theoretical perspectives can be considered complements to each other. The phishing/phools perspective arguably downplays the ethical responsibilities of business decision makers. This perspective does not recognize that business decisions are too often made in an excessively self-interested manner and that such businesses are often quick to take advantage of customer weaknesses, whether or not the market is very competitive. On the other hand, the dual motive view can be faulted for not recognizing customers' poor decision making and customers' inability to understand or appreciate what is really good for them. In light of these contrasting viewpoints, it would make sense to integrate these two perspectives. Certainly, these two perspectives should both be an important part of BE – a BE that aspires to have humanistic values, and that aspires to make the economy function more humanely. It is unlikely that an economy will become more humane in its functioning in the absence of a theoretical perspective that incorporates a humane vision of how the market economy can best function and how the dysfunctions can be corrected.

Paul Zak, oxytocin, and economics

Paul Zak is a well-known economist who appreciates that the softer, more intangible side of human behavior is very important for determining how well a society or an economy performs. Thus, it is not so surprising that Zak discovered the importance of oxytocin and its relation to economic functioning. What is oxytocin? "Oxytocin is a small molecule, or 'peptide' [in humans] that serves as both a neurotransmitter, sending signals within the brain, and a hormone, carrying messages in the bloodstream" (Zak 2012, p. 23). Oxytocin is known to control the onset of a woman's labor during childbirth, and it regulates the flow of her milk during breast-feeding. What Zak has emphasized in his research is that there is a direct link between the amount of oxytocin in humans' blood and brains and humans' concern for others, that is, people's mutual sympathy or empathy (p. 24). Oxytocin is important for helping "humans walk the line between competition and cooperation" (p. 24). Most importantly, oxytocin fosters trust. Oxytocin surges in a person's bloodstream when an individual is shown a sign of trust and/or when something engages a person's sympathies and they experience empathy (p. xvii).

Although Zak is an accomplished economist, he has in later years also become a neuroscientist. For example, he and two colleagues did research that resulted in an article entitled "The Neurobiology of Trust" which was published in the *Annals of the New York Academy of Science* in 2004. This research "examined the role of oxytocin in facilitating trust" (Zak et al. 2004, p. 224). Their findings confirmed the hypothesis that "oxytocin [levels in a person's blood] would rise in response to a social signal of trust and that an increase in oxytocin would be associated with trustworthy behavior" (p. 224). According to Zak, this is very important for understanding not only human relationships but for understanding business productivity and the functioning of economies. What Zak discovered is that among "interpersonal factors affecting prosperity, the most compelling . . . [is] trust" (Zak 2012, p. 22). Trust is important because it is crucial for "being able to enforce contracts, [and] being able to rely on others to deliver what they promise and not cheat or steal' (p. 22). In Zak's view, trust "is a more powerful factor in a country's economic development than education, access to resources – anything" (p. 22). Further, the marketplace makes people more moral, not less. Trade supports a virtuous productivity cycle involving oxytocin (pp. 159–160). In this prosperity cycle, oxytocin leads to empathy, leading to morality, leading to trust, leading to prosperity, leading back to oxytocin (and the cycle continues) (p. 160). According to Zak, "moral behavior actually increases the efficiency and profitability of trade," and prosperity (a larger economic pie) "if reasonably well distributed, reduces stress and increases trust" (p. 160). There are, of course, as Zak recognizes, a variety of factors that can get in the way of creating the kind of good relationships that produce continuing prosperity with accompanying high levels of oxytocin. What is clear in Zak's view is that if the economy and human relations go well, this will lead to high levels of oxytocin that will help sustain the virtuous cycle. The goal, of course, is not high levels of oxytocin, but high oxytocin can, among other things, serve as a valuable indicator that the economy and business activity are doing well.

Conclusion

Economics needs to be more humanistic, and this means it needs more theorizing that connects with core human values, theorizing that helps understand why things go wrong, and why socio-economies malfunction. It therefore needs to be able to give us good ideas about what we need to do to improve socio-economic functioning. Arguably, it would be good if more BE writings were oriented to these humanistic concerns. BE does, of course, need to be scientific in all the usual ways. It needs descriptive theorizing and good empirical work. But it also needs a kind of normative theorizing that is connected to deeper understandings of human nature, even wisdom. Thus, it sometimes needs a high level of generalization that attempts to capture those higher levels of truth. But, of course, achieving that is not easy, and there are no guarantees that aspirations to wisdom will be realized.

NOTES

1 This human brain structure and circuitry evolved over millions of years. The three evolved brain modules or neural assemblies constitute a hierarchy in which the whole is greater than the sum of its parts (MacLean 1990, pp. 8–9; see also Wilson 2006, pp. 628–629). It is important to note that MacLean's contribution is integrative in nature, not reductive. As such he provides an overall evolutionary phylogenetic perspective on brain functioning that may not coincide precisely with findings of scientists operating in reductive and comparative structural functional modes. This is to be expected and does not invalidate his invaluable contribution. Even if it does not link exactly with evolutionary history, MacLean's conception of the triune brain can be seen as a powerful way to organize the functioning of the brain and relate it to the evolution of brain physiology.

2 The human motivation deriving from the paleomammalian brain is empathy, other-interest, or other regarding. These three terms are used in a roughly synonymous way.

References

Akerlof, George A. and Shiller, Robert J. 2015. *Phishing for Phools: The Economics of Manipulation and Deception*. Princeton: Princeton University Press.

Blinder, Alan S. 2013. *After the Music Stopped: The Financial Crisis, the Response, and the Work Ahead*. New York: Penguin Books.

Cory Jr, Gerald A. 1999. *The Reciprocal Modular Brain in Economics and Politics: Shaping the Rational and Moral Basis of Organization, Exchange and Choice*. New York: Kluwer Academic.

Doidge, Norman. 2007. *The Brain That Changes Itself: Stories of Personal Triumph from the Frontiers of Brain Science*. London: Penguin Group.

Lynne, Gary D., Czap, Natalia, Czap, Hans and Burbach, Mark. 2015. "Empathy Conservation: Toward Avoiding the Tragedy of the Commons," *Review of Behavioral Economics*, forthcoming.

MacLean, Paul. 1990. *The Triune Brain in Evolution: Role in Paleocerebral Functions*. New York: Plenum.

McCloskey, Deirdre. 2006. *The Bourgeois Virtues: Ethics for an Age of Commerce*. Chicago: The University of Chicago Press.

Smith, Adam. 1776. *An Inquiry into the Nature and the Causes of the Wealth of Nations*. E. Cannan (ed) New York: Modern Library, 1937.

Smith, Adam. 1759/1790. *The Theory of Moral Sentiments*. 6th Edition. D.D. Raphael and A.L. Macfie (eds) Indianapolis, IN: Liberty Classics, 1982.

Tomer, John F. 2012. "Brain Physiology, Egoistic and Empathic Motivation, and Brain Plasticity: Toward a More Human Economics," *World Economic Review*, 1(1), 76–90.

Tomer, John F. 2016. *Integrating Human Capital with Human Development: The Path to a More Productive and Humane Economy*. New York: Palgrave Macmillan.

Wilson, D. R. 2006. "The Evolutionary Neuroscience of Human Reciprocal Sociality: A Basic Outline for Economists," *Journal of Socio-Economics*, 35, 626–633.

Zak, Paul J.; Kurzban, Robert; and Matzner, William T. 2004. "The Neurobiology of Trust," *Annals New York Academy of Science*, 1032, 224–227.

Zak, Paul J. 2012. *The Moral Molecule: How Trust Works*. New York: Penguin.

14 Behavioral economic trends

Introduction

Behavioral economics, like any scientific discipline, changes over time. New research results in the discovery of new truths and leads to new perspectives. Young researchers enter the ranks and may see the world quite differently from seasoned researchers. Some of the young are inclined to do normal science in the established scientific tradition. Others will be inclined to follow more radical and innovative paths. Some research will be in line with prevailing political and social norms; some will challenge conventional norms. It is hard to predict how a science will evolve, whether research progress will be largely conventional or will have a revolutionary element. So I cannot confidently predict the future of behavioral economics (BE). What I can do is point out some significant new research. This new research may be indicative of what will occur in the future. That is because it is likely that researchers working in the near future will follow in the footsteps of those who have experienced success and accordingly gained recognition for their research in the recent past. Below I point out and explain about some important new research efforts that quite plausibly are indicative of important BE trends. I make no claims to have made a comprehensive survey of recent BE research.

The political or ideological factor

Political or ideological factors can influence both the research that is attempted and the findings of that research. Consider research regarding the public policies known as nudges. Initially, research advocating and explaining nudges was very widely accepted. Now in some quarters there is a more skeptical or critical view of nudges. The book entitled *Nudge Theory in Action* edited by Sherzod Abdukadirov (2016) is an example of research that takes such a critical and ideological view. At the heart of this book is the neoclassical assumption that people are rational or with effort can be rational; and, therefore, they should be left alone to deal with their problems and failures. This is because people experiencing difficulties can be expected to wrestle with their problems and consequently will frequently find viable solutions. According to the authors, this is much better than reliance on government nudges, nudges that often involve violations of ethical precepts, particularly precepts that involve moral rules against coercion and manipulation. The authors of the articles in Abdukadirov's book almost uniformly share a strong bias or partiality towards market activity and against government activity. Since the advocates of nudges have typically emphasized the use of nudges by government, this book's authors are inclined to oppose the nudge idea. In their minds, nudges are associated strongly with regulation, strong forms of paternalism, use of taxes and subsidies as incentives, etc. Reflecting their political and ideological leanings, the book's authors have difficulty understanding how people in accord with BE findings could have psychological biases that lead them to make decisions that are neither in their best interests nor in the interests of their community, region, or country. The authors also tend to have excessive skepticism about policymakers' ability to design effective, ethical nudges. Further, the authors have difficulty understanding social problems, particularly when these problems have not only an individual dimension but also a societal one. Obesity is an example. The authors tend to understand obesity's causes as stemming primarily from a lack of individual rationality and self-control. They have trouble understanding that obesity has very important socio-economic and social value dimensions. In other words, they fail to grasp that obesity involves socio-economic dysfunction. What I suspect is that more research in this critical, ideological vein can be expected.

Raj Chetty's approach to behavioral economics

Raj Chetty is a relatively young economist whose research work has been extremely productive. Therefore, it is interesting to examine both his general approach to BE and how his approach has worked in a number of his important research projects. Most importantly, Chetty approaches BE from a pragmatic, policy-oriented perspective:

> Instead of posing the central research question as 'are the assumptions of the neoclassical economic model valid,' the pragmatic approach starts from a policy question – for example, 'how can we increase savings rates?' – and

incorporates behavioral factors to the extent that they improve empirical
prediction and policy decisions. (Chetty 2015, p. 1)

Chetty is very much in favor of incorporating BE into his analyses.
However, he believes that his pragmatic perspective to BE "represents
a natural progression of (rather than a challenge to) neoclassical economic methods" (p. 1). Chetty also believes that BE "offers *new policy
tools* that can be used to influence behavior" (p. 1). In addition, Chetty
finds that "BE can yield better predictions about the effects of existing policies" and that BE "generates new welfare implications" (p. 2).
It is important to note that in a number of Chetty's recent applied
microeconomic studies, he uses a "big data" approach that involves
using administrative datasets with millions of observations. This ties
in with the trend in economics to increasingly become an empirical
science (p. 5). In accord with this, Chetty believes "economic theories will [increasingly] be shaped more directly by evidence" and that
the "pragmatic approach to BE . . . may become even more prevalent"
(p. 5). Thus, there are quite a few good reasons to believe that other
economists will find it worthwhile to follow in Chetty's footsteps.

Several years ago Chetty, along with a number of his American and
Danish research colleagues, embarked on a study of the retirement
savings of employees (Chetty et al. 2014). The issue that prompted
this research is the concern that many people do not save enough
for their retirement. In light of this concern, policymakers are interested in what the government can do to raise household savings rates.
Neoclassical economics (NE) thinking on this subject has emphasized
the use of incentives for saving. Thus, "the traditional approach to
increasing retirement savings is to subsidize saving in retirement
accounts" (p. 10). In the U.S., this has meant that income placed in
qualifying retirement savings accounts is exempt from income taxation. Does this NE-oriented policy work to raise savings? Previous
research findings on this have suffered because of a lack of sufficient
data and because the NE models used do not do well at predicting
observed savings behavior (p. 10). The data problem was solved when
Chetty and his colleagues were able to gain access to data on the savings of all Danish citizens from 1995 to 2000; this dataset included 41
million observations (p. 10). Of particular interest was the fact that in
1999, the Danish government reduced the tax deduction on income
deposited in the pensions. The researchers found that subsequently
aggregate retirement savings dropped sharply, appearing to confirm
NE expectation. However, on further investigation, it was found that

many individuals (about 81 percent) left their pension contributions unchanged. The other 19 percent of the individuals almost entirely stopped contributing to their pension savings. This contradicts the NE model. It indicates that 81 percent of individuals are "passive" or unresponsive savers, while the other 19 percent are "active" savers (p. 11). Next Chetty and colleagues assessed whether the 19 percent of individuals who stopped their pension contributions reduced their total saving or shifted their pension money to other accounts. They found that almost all of the reduction in pension contributions was offset by increased savings in other types of accounts (pp. 11–12). To sum up, the researchers found that most retirement savers are passive, although a small minority ("sophisticated" retirement savers) are active. This does not support NE savings theory. NE theory assumes that all people optimize. In the wake of the changed tax incentive for saving, NE theory certainly predicts that all individuals will respond to the reduced incentive, and accordingly, lower their savings. What is the lesson to be learned from these results? It is that:

> the standard tools suggested by neoclassical models are not very successful ... in increasing savings rates because they appear to induce only a small group of financially sophisticated individuals to respond, and these individuals simply shift assets between accounts. These results naturally lead to the question of whether other policy tools – perhaps those that directly target passive savers – can be more effective in increasing saving. (Chetty et al. 2014, p. 12)

Which policy tools make the most sense in increasing retirement savings rates? As Chapter 7 has explained, increased savings can be nudged by making employees' enrollment in their savings plans automatic, i.e., making employees' enrollment in the plan the default, but also allowing employees the right to opt-out of enrollment in the plan. It turns out that there is a great deal of research evidence that savings plan defaults have a large impact on how much employees contribute to retirement accounts, despite leaving individuals' incentives unchanged (Chetty 2015, p. 12). According to recent research, when employers' adopt such defaults, it results in increased employee participation in 401(k) pension plans from 20 percent to 80 percent at the point of hire. To verify these findings, "it is critical to determine whether these larger retirement contributions come at the expense of less saving in non-retirement accounts or actually induce individuals to consume less" (p. 12). Chetty et al. (2014) are able to resolve this problem because the Danish data they use contain information on savings in *all* accounts" of these employees (p. 12). If the employees "are 'passive savers' who are inattentive to their retirement plans and simply follow the default option," automatic enrollment will result in them increasing their retirement savings (p. 13). "The broader [pragmatic] lesson of this [research] work is that defaults make it feasible to achieve outcomes that cannot be achieved with subsidies" (p. 14). This understanding only makes sense in the context of a behavioral model in which individuals' choices are passive, i.e., not responsive or optimizing.

Similar to his work with retirement savings, Chetty's empirical BE research includes the following topics: 1) the importance of simplification with respect to individuals' choice of health insurance plans, 2) how assistance to college applicants in completing their applications can significantly raise college attendance rates, 3) the framing of teacher incentives so that students' failure to improve their performance causes teachers to give back bonuses that had been announced in advance, 4) sending letters to households informing them of their energy usage relative to their neighbors so that the social comparison might stimulate them to conserve energy (Chetty 2015, p. 16). In each of these types of research, the "goal is to evaluate the efficacy of [the] new policy tools ... rather than test specific assumptions of NE or behavioral models" (p. 16).

Conducting online experiments

Chapter 10 of this book, which is entitled "The Empirical Methods of Behavioral Economics," deals with a wide range of empirical methods used by behavioral economists, particularly the experimental methods taking place in laboratories. Not mentioned there is a new experimental method that involves experiments that take place online. In these experiments, there is no physical laboratory, and there is no place that experimental subjects come to. An article entitled "Conducting Interactive Experiments Online" by Arechar, Gachter, and Molleman (AGM) (2016) provides a good explanation of how such experiments work and how they differ from laboratory experiments.

To conduct online experiments, researchers must employ online labor markets such as Amazon Mechanical Turk (MTurk) that are increasingly popular with experimental researchers (Arechar et al. 2016, p. 2). "With their large and diverse pools of people ready to promptly perform tasks for pay, these markets present researchers with new opportunities to recruit participants for experiments" (p. 2). Based on careful comparisons of laboratory experiments with online experiments, the data obtained online has been found to be as reliable as that obtained from the laboratory (p. 2).

In the past, behavioral online research has been largely limited to non-interactive decision making tasks or one-shot games with simultaneous decisions. Very recently, researchers have begun to do interactive online experiments in which a group of participants interacts with each other for more than one repetition (p. 2). Such interactive participation presents novel challenges during the whole process of an experiment. One of the significant challenges is participant dropout. "While in the physical laboratory subjects rarely leave a session, online experiments are more prone to facing dropouts which affect both the participant who is dropping out and their interaction partners" (p. 2).

To compare an online experiment with a laboratory experiment, AGM have used a repeated public goods game. The comparison involves a fairly long and complex experiment with two experimental conditions each with 10 periods, and there are new instructions after the first 10 periods (Arechar et al. 2016, p. 3). AGM find that the basic patterns of behavior are very similar for both the online and laboratory versions of the experiment. The most important result of the comparison is that subject dropouts are higher in the online version of the experiment. Despite this, the "results suggest that online interactive experiments can be a reliable tool for collecting . . . valid data and hence are a valuable complement to the physical laboratory" (p. 3).

The public goods game used in the comparison was a 10-period game in which all participants were assigned to groups consisting of four members, and each member simultaneously received an endowment, e.g., 20 points, and had to decide how many of the points to keep and how many to contribute to a group project (the public good). After all of the members had made their decisions, the total contribution to the public good is multiplied by 1.6 and distributed equally among all the members (Arechar et al. 2016, p. 4). There is a social dilemma involved because overall earnings are highest when each group member contributes all their points to the public good. At the same time, any individual can maximize their earnings by contributing zero points (p. 4).

The online sample of participants were recruited via MTurk. Show-up fees for online subjects were $1. The average age of online participants was 31.5, and 38.1 percent of them were females. The average earnings of online subjects for one research experience were $6.69 paid via MTurk (Arechar et al. 2016, p. 5). As indicated earlier, MTurk is a very large online labor market; it offers an active pool of over 500,000 workers (p. 16). MTurk "workers" browse a published list of scheduled online research opportunities and decide which of them they will make themselves available for. Researchers are able to conduct large-scale experiments because of the large size of the pool of workers who are ready to perform these research tasks for pay (p. 6). As mentioned above, "the severest problem for online interactive experiments, and the largest discrepancy with laboratory experiments is *attrition* (subject dropout)" (p. 10). This is because there is no easy way to keep participants from leaving a session. Some dropouts occur because there can be a variety of delays in the progress of an experiment. These delays may discourage online workers so that some withdraw from participating in an experiment that has already started (p. 11).

Despite relatively high subject dropout rates in the online experiments, the dropout factor was not a big issue with respect to the experimental data. The individuals who dropped out were not significantly different from those who did not (Arechar et al. 2016, p. 17). "Attrition though a significant nuisance in online experiments did not compromise the internal validity of [the] data because attrition was unrelated to what happened in the experiments" (p. 18).

Because of the relatively favorable experimental results experienced by online researchers, it is to be expected that much more online research will occur in the future.

Nudging to improve health

An increasing number of articles and books are appearing related to nudging and health care. There are a couple of good reasons for this. One is the growing appreciation of the importance of nudging for health care:

> If people didn't smoke, drank less, ate healthier diets and were more active, the huge burden of chronic diseases such as cancer, heart disease, and type 2 diabetes would be much reduced. The prospect of being able to nudge populations into changing their behavior has generated great interest among policymakers worldwide. (Marteau 2011, p. 263)

The problem that people have is that although they value their health, they persist in behaviors that contribute to their health problems. This is partly because people are not inclined to use what cognitive capacity they have to think carefully in a goal-oriented manner about how they need to behave in order to attain high health. The other part of the problem is that people are inclined to rely on their automatic, affective (system 2) thinking (p. 263). In other words, their decision making is too often driven by immediate feelings and triggered by their environments.

Nudging can help people improve their health behavior without involving government legislation, regulation, and interventions that alter incentives. That is the appeal of nudging; "it proposes a set of seemingly simple, low cost solutions that do not require legislation and can be applied to a wide array of problems arising from our behavior" (p. 263). There has been a rapid growth of nudging initiatives that are informed by behavioral findings. In the U.S. these initiatives enlist such tools as disclosure, warnings, and default rules, and they can be found in many areas involving fuel economy, energy efficiency, environmental protection, health care, and obesity" (Sunstein 2014, p. 12). In the United Kingdom, the efforts of their Behavioral Insights Team"draw on insights from a growing body of academic research in the fields of BE and psychology which show how often subtle changes to the way in which decisions are framed can have big impacts on how people respond to them" (p. 12). Many other nations are now interested in nudging and are initiating government programs to foster nudging efforts (pp. 12–13). As mentioned in Chapter 7, a 2014 study found that "136 countries around the world have incorporated behavioral sciences in some aspect of public policy, and 51 'have developed centrally directed policy initiatives ... influenced by the new behavioral sciences'" (Thaler 2015, p. 344). In light of this, it is not surprising that the interest in nudging to improve health is growing and an increasing amount of research related to nudging health is occurring.

Hopefully, the future nudge research and future nudge initiatives will follow the wisdom of Richard Thaler. He has reminded us that nudges are merely tools (Thaler 2015, p. 345). "Businesses or governments with bad intentions can use the findings of the behavioral sciences for self-serving purposes, at the expense of the people who have been nudged" (p. 345). Let's make sure that we "nudge for good," i.e., nudging to make the world a better place (p. 307). And that involves "carefully selecting nudges based on science, and then subjecting these interventions to rigorous tests" (p. 345).

Should economists be plumbers?

Esther Duflo (2017) has recently argued that too often economists have an overly narrow conception of their role when they attempt to help governments design new policies and regulations. This is important because economists are increasingly getting such opportunities to help governments around the world. Economists have typically thought of themselves as scientists who are concerned with the big picture or broad design. It is, however, becoming more and more clear that to achieve success in their governmental engagements, economists are going to have to take broader responsibility and "focus on many details about which their models and theories do not give much guidance" (p. 1). There are two reasons for this:

> First, it turns out that policy makers rarely have the time or the inclination to focus on . . . [the details], and will tend to decide on how to address them based on hunches, without much regard for evidence. Figuring all of this out is therefore not something that economists can just leave to policy makers after delivering their report . . . . Second, details that we as economists might consider relatively uninteresting are in fact extraordinarily important in determining the final impact of a policy or a regulation, while some of the theoretical issues we worry about most may not be that relevant. (Duflo 2017, p. 1)

Here is a key difficulty:

> Paying attention to the details of policy requires a mindset that is slightly different from that which graduate school instills in economists . . . . Economists . . . tend to think in 'machine mode': they want to find out the button that will get the machine started . . ., the 'root cause' of the problem. (Duflo 2017, pp. 2–3)

Also, economists have a strong tendency to think that paying attention to many details and complications is work more suitable for someone far below their pay grade (p. 3). Consequently, what is needed according to Duflo is that economists should have more of a "plumbing mindset." "The economist-plumber stands on the shoulder of scientists and engineers . . . . She is more concerned about 'how' to do things than about 'what' to do" (p. 3). Engineers in contrast start with general principles and apply them to specific situations. "The plumber goes . . . further than the engineer: she installs the machine in the real world, carefully watches what happens, and then tinkers as needed" to work out the details (p. 5). When economists fail to step into the roles of either engineers or plumbers when needed, they fall into traps related to ideology, ignorance, and inertia. Then "policy makers tend to design schemes based on the ideology of the time, in complete ignorance of the reality of the field, and once these policies are in place, they just stay in place" (p. 13).

Among the reasons why plumbing matters for public policy is that:

> the citizens (or the supposed beneficiaries of the policies) are humans, with conflicting objectives, limited information sets, limited attention, and limited willpower. This means that the specific way that policies are presented and implemented will potentially have tremendous influence on whether they will work or not. (Duflo 2017, p. 15)

Another reason why plumbing matters concerns those whose job it is to implement policies. These government workers are humans too. Accordingly, they also have many of the same limitations as citizens, and they probably do not have much incentive to work very hard or in the best interests of the ultimate beneficiaries.

In addition to her arguments for why economists should behave more like plumbers, Duflo has provided many examples of how economic plumbing can be important and helpful. Her examples include: 1) cities in the developing world lacking access to home water, 2) difficulties designing the health exchanges for the Affordable Care Act (U.S.), 3) designing markets including incentive schemes and government regulation, 4) changing the way students are assigned to schools (Boston), 5) fixing the problems associated with the Indonesian government's rice distribution scheme, and 6) trying to improve the situation involving rising health care costs and non-communicable diseases in the state of Kerala, India (Duflo 2017). In essence, Duflo believes that "plumbing should be an inherent part of our profession: we [economists] are well prepared for it, reasonably good at it, and it is how we make ourselves useful" fixing many problems around the world (p. 31).

Conclusion

This chapter has provided a number of examples of types of research that are indicative of current BE trends. There is a lot of BE research of different kinds occurring, as BE continues to grow and evolve in many directions. The research examples provided above are certainly of interest but are only a small sample of what is happening in BE these days.

References

Abdukadirov, Sherzod (ed) 2016. *Nudge Theory in Action: Behavioral Design in Policy and Markets*. New York: Palgrave Macmillan.

Arechar, Antonio A., Gachter, Simon and Molleman, Lucas. 2016. "Conducting Interactive Experiments Online," Available on the Social Science Research Network, December.

Chetty, Raj. 2015. "Behavioral Economics and Public Policy: A Pragmatic Perspective," National Bureau of Economic Research Working Paper 20928, Prepared for the Richard T. Ely Lecture (American Economic Association).

Chetty, Raj et al. 2014. "Active vs. Passive Decisions and Crowd-out in Retirement Savings Accounts: Evidence from Denmark," *Quarterly Journal of Economics*, 129(3), 1141–1219.

Duflo, Esther. 2017. "The Economist as Plumber," Paper based on the Ely lecture delivered at the American Economic Association meeting, January.

Marteau, Theresa. 2011. "Judging Nudging: Can Nudging Improve Population Health?," *British Medical Journal*, January 29, 342, 263–265.

Sunstein, Cass R. 2014. *Why Nudge? The Politics of Libertarian Paternalism*. Connecticut: Yale University Press.

Thaler, Richard H. 2015. *Misbehaving: The Making of Behavioral Economics*. New York: Norton.

15 Conclusion

Chapter 2 raised the question of whether behavioral economics (BE) is a new paradigm, possibly a superior paradigm, that might succeed neoclassical economics (NE), the current paradigm. Chapter 2 also considered how the scientific practices of BE differ from those of NE. Clearly, there are fundamental differences between BE and NE. There are, for example, sharp differences between the NE behavioral assumptions and those of BE. And the scientific methods of BE and NE are also very different. NE emphasizes a positivistic philosophy and rigorous mathematical methods. BE, on the other hand, rejects positivism, strongly accepts interdisciplinary social science, and finds much less use for mathematics. In general, NE is much more narrow, rigid, intolerant, mechanical, separate, and individualistic than BE. Based on this comparison, there is a strong argument that the scientific practices of the emergent BE constitute a new paradigm.

Let's consider the overall situation regarding the scientific changes that have occurred and seem to be occurring. After my review of all that has been happening in recent years, the prospect for paradigm change does not seem clear at all. To get a better idea about this, it is useful to think about arraying all behavioral economists along a spectrum. On the low end of the spectrum would be economists who have adopted only a relatively small amount of the scientific practices associated with BE. On the high end would be economists who have adopted a very large amount of the scientific practices of BE. One of the economists on the low end of the spectrum would surely be Matthew Rabin (2002), a leading behavioral researcher. He has expressed the view that the main difference between NE and BE is that the assumptions of BE have greater psychological realism than those of NE. Rabin is for the most part not critical of NE methods. Economists such as Rabin like their psychological realism with a large dose of NE methods. Others like the followers of Herbert Simon are in favor of a BE that is fundamentally different from NE, i.e., a BE that is different along many dimensions. These days there clearly are many varieties of behavioral economists.

Most behavioral economists, of course, would be located somewhere in the middle of the spectrum. Two examples follow.

Consider the BE orientation of Raj Chetty, the young Harvard economics professor. As mentioned in Chapter 14, Chetty has a pragmatic perspective regarding the difference between BE and NE. His view is that "BE represents a natural progression of (rather than a challenge to) NE methods" (Chetty 2015, p. 1). He believes that "BE is better viewed as a part of all economists' toolkit (like other tools in applied theory) rather than as a separate subfield [or paradigm]" (p. 37). Chetty finds BE very useful "to the extent that . . . [it] improves empirical predictions and policy decisions" (p. 1). Despite his use of BE tools, Chetty believes that "the neoclassical model remains the benchmark for most economic applications" (p. 1).

Richard Thaler (2016, p. 1) is a more thorough going behavioral economist than Chetty, but he does not believe that BE represents a "paradigm shifting revolution." In his view, "the methodology of BE returns economic thinking to the way it began with Adam Smith" (p. 1). Thaler emphasizes that there are "historical precedents for utilizing a psychologically realistic depiction of the representative agent" (p. 1). In his view, the significance of BE is that it considers the important role of the "supposedly irrelevant factors" (factors typically deriving from non-economic social science) in its models, whereas NE does not. According to Thaler, if everyone [all economists] were to include all the factors [including the supposedly irrelevant ones] that determine economic behaviors in their models, then the field of BE would no longer need to exist (p. 1). In this event, economics would then be "the kind of open-minded, intuitively motivated discipline that was invented by Adam Smith" (p. 19).

As suggested by the above, BE as it exists today may no doubt have some potential for giving birth to a new full-fledged paradigm, but it does not seem close to realizing that potential in the near future. The great diversity of opinions and scientific practices among all economists would seem to rule out a scientific revolution for now.

References

Chetty, Raj. 2015. "Behavioral Economics and Public Policy: A Pragmatic Perspective," National Bureau of Economic Research Working Paper 20928, Prepared for the Richard T. Ely Lecture (American Economic Association).

Rabin, Matthew. 2002. "A Perspective on Psychology and Economics," *European Economic Review*, 46, 657–685.

Thaler, Richard H. 2016. "Behavioral Economics: Past, Present, and Future," Available on the Social Science Research Network, May 27.

Index

Titles in the **Elgar Advanced Introductions** series include:

International Political Economy
Benjamin J. Cohen

The Austrian School of Economics
Randall G. Holcombe

Cultural Economics
Ruth Towse

Law and Development
Michael J. Trebilcock and Mariana Mota Prado

International Humanitarian Law
Robert Kolb

International Tax Law
Reuven S. Avi-Yonah

Post Keynesian Economics
J.E. King

International Intellectual Property
Susy Frankel and Daniel J. Gervais

Public Management and Administration
Christopher Pollitt

Organised Crime
Leslie Holmes

Nationalism
Liah Greenfeld

Social Policy
Daniel Béland and Rianne Mahon

Consumer Behavior Analysis
Gordon Foxall

Entrepreneurial Finance
Hans Landström

International Conflict and Security Law
Nigel D. White

Comparative Constitutional Law
Mark Tushnet

International Human Rights Law
Dinah L. Shelton

Entrepreneurship
Robert D. Hisrich

International Trade Law
Michael J. Trebilcock

Public Policy
B. Guy Peters

The Law of International Organizations
Jan Klabbers

International Environmental Law
Ellen Hey

International Sales Law
Clayton P. Gillette

Corporate Venturing
Robert D. Hisrich

Public Choice
Randall G. Holcombe

Private Law
Jan M. Smits

Globalisation
Jonathan Michie

Behavioral Economics
John F. Tomer